MW01712958

ACROSS HER HEART

ACROSS HER HEART

S.N. MEZA

House of Freedom Publishings

Welland, Ontario

Book cover and illustrations created by Sarah Meza Designs. See www.facebook.com/sarahmezadesigns or Instagram @sarahmezadesigns for more artwork and contact information.

The Fell Types are digitally reproduced by Igino Marini. www.iginomarini.com, used with permission.

To the Marked and the Markless,
Who have been giving ceaselessly with their hands, their heart,
and their mind;
May you uncover rest, may you abide in joy, and may you
unveil your true identity,
in who the Artist says you are.

Contents

Soundtrack for Across Her Heart

How blessed am I, that I am married to a composer, musician, and a creator!

When I spoke to him during the third draft, asking him to create music that captured the emotions of each part, without hesitation he said yes.

Within a few days he showed me what he had been spending hours in solitude on; I was left speechless.

One evening, playing songs together in the basement of my parent's home, I closed my eyes and asked him to play for me. He started the piece with this simple melody, but as the notes reached my ears it felt as if the melody was the soul of the book. I cried out, "That's Annona! You must work that melody into each part!" His face showed exasperation, but luckily for him he had only started the first part of six.

You may want to read each Part of the book, and listen to the soundtrack after it has been read. Thus, you will be able to pick out thematic sounds and melodies that are derived from that section. Or, you may read each Part with the corresponding soundtrack playing in the background, or even listen to the specific Part before you read. Either way, we invite you to listen along. My husband is a musician. He is a creator. Working on this project with him has bonded our creative gifting together, and I am grateful and continue to be blown away by his musical gifts and talents.

Soundtrack for Her Hands, her Heart, and her Mind

The soundtrack is streamed on all major music platforms and is available for purchase by searching *Jairo Meza* or *Across Her Heart Soundtrack*.

Why Across Her Heart Exists

"So shall my word be that goes out from my mouth; it shall not return to me empty, but it shall accomplish that which I purpose, and shall succeed in the thing for which I sent it."
Isaiah 55:11

I sat on the airplane destined for Toronto Pearson International Airport. Staring at the worn and heavily finger-printed mini-screen fixed to the back of the seat in front of me, I watched a recorded concert of the Lumineers playing a live show in New York City. I was desperate for the music to distract me from my harrowing anxieties. My stomach wrenched with guilt, tears stung my eyes. *What have I done?* I kept asking myself. I felt the bile rising in my throat, and I desperately swallowed to keep it down. My husband, Jairo, sat stoically beside me, our fingers interlaced as he squeezed my grip, a tear slipped past my cheek. My daughter, Abigail, not yet a year old, was in my arms, restlessly gnawing on the toy we had given her.

What have I done? My mind unravelled into a panic. I wanted to shriek at the pilot, demand that he turn the plane around and instead take me back to what I identified as home.

From the time I was fourteen, my life was wrapped in visions of travelling across seas, spending myself on behalf of the hungry, and satisfying the needs of the oppressed. It wouldn't be until I was sixteen that I would have my first experience in cross-cultural service trips, and finally when I turned twenty-three, I moved to Honduras. I was ready to give my life to furthering God's Kingdom. The world behind me, His cross before me, no turning back, no turning back.

In that moment, as the salty tears raced down my cheek and fell unto my lap, leaving dark splotches on my jeans, the severity and finality of our decision to leave Honduras hit me profoundly for the first time. This would be the first time in three years I would not have a return ticket that would deliver me back to the place I called home. This was a one-way trip with a new destiny before me—one I wanted no part of.

As pain and failure penetrated against the weakened barriers of my heart, I was unaware of how severely this question that rang in my head would affect me: *what have I done?* It would be the resounding question that would clash in my mind for the next six months, tormenting me in moments of silence, lingering on an infinite loop anytime there was a pause. Unaware of how truly dark it would become, I altogether surrendered myself to the misery of failing my calling and having to start over again. I had no sense of identity apart from my calling, from my ability to serve with my hands, my heart, and my mind. *Who was I if I wasn't serving?*

This book is not about the glory of following your calling. Nor is it about the glorious peace and love that is inevitably experienced when you give yourself for the betterment of others. This book is for those who gave themselves as best as they perceived to follow God's calling on their life, but failed in the process, and were left to pick up the fragments of their broken dreams. It is written for those of us who may have made grave errors along the way and who were engaged in the entanglements of sin and foolish behaviours, which merely obscured our grief and complicated our anger. The shame heightening our loss, we held ourselves to a higher level of accountability than others, refusing to allow ourselves any grace.

This is for those of us who have lost track of who we are and what we are called to do, who feel that our dreams are dead—but maybe, *just maybe*, we cling fiercely to the vaguest belief that the dream may be resurrected.

We are the ones who have grown accustomed to the seasons of the earth, knowing full well that our callings rest beneath deep layers of soil: the soil itself full of sorrow and besieged by darkness. However, as is the seasons of the earth, we trust that it ultimately has to—*it must*—burst forth. This is for those of us who refuse to believe that God is done with us, who hold fast on to hope, even when we are surrounded by storms. It is for those of us who have experienced pain, experienced difficulties and trials unfathomable, but nevertheless have the words *your grace is sufficient for me* on the tips of our tongue.

It took a lot of time, solitude, and prayer to believe God was not finished with me. I had never encountered such darkness and anger, which came as a result of genuinely believing that my life was meaningless, as I did in the first six months of my return to Canada. That period of darkness was a stage to which I wish to never return. But, through and even *amidst* the darkness, God met me where I was, restoring me into an understanding of His grace, truth, and love that is higher and more beautiful than I could have ever understood before.

I do not know what your story is, but my hope and prayer is that you discover who you are in Jesus—in who God says you are: a child of God (John 1:12), adopted by his grace (Ephesians 1:5), who has power, love, and a sound mind (2 Timothy 1:7), and may approach God with freedom and confidence (Ephesians 3:12). He is not done with you or the calling He has instilled in you; He is *never* finished with you. Allow the God who resurrects *even death* to breathe life into the embers of your calling, producing hope and bringing new life back to your dreams.

Name Ledger & Meaning

Annona (ah-no-nah) *Latin Origin: Of the Harvest* – This is her story about her Marking.

Painter – Dwells among, He who gives the Marking.

Sculptor – He who Was, Is, and Is to come.

Potter – He who sacrificed Himself for the Marked and the Markless.

Artist – A Name of love, used interchangeably for Painter, Sculptor, and Potter.

Akim (ah-keem) *Hebrew Origin: God will Establish* – Elder Harvester in the Land of Rolling Hills.

Jore *Hebrew Origin: God will Uplift* – Planter in the Land of Rolling Hills.

Manasses *Hebrew Origin: To Forget* – Harvester in the Land of Rolling Hills.

Osias *Hebrew Origin: Salvation*– Marking unknown.

List of Characters and Meaning

Adah *Hebrew Origin: Beautiful, Ornament* – Provider in Guardian's Ridge.

Kachash (kaw-khash) *Hebrew Origin: Failure*– Master of Failure.

Perispaó (per-ee-spah'-o) *Hebrew Origin: Distraction* – Master of Distraction.

Angō (ang-oh) *Hebrew Origin: Anxiety* – Master of Anxiety.

Telaah (tel-aw-aw') (The Brothers) *Hebrew Origin: Chaos* – Master of Chaos.

Peirasmos (pi-ras-mos') (The Brothers) *Hebrew Origin: Suffering* – Master of Suffering.

Mirmah (meer-maw') *Hebrew Origin: Deception* – Master of Deception.

Yirah (yir-aw') *Hebrew Origin: Fear* – Master of Fear.

Map of the Ends of the Earth

OBSERT'S
STONE
LAND of ROLLING
HILLS
ENDS of THE
EARTH
LAND of SAND
LAND
of HEAT
GUARDIAN'S
RIDGE
LAND of FOUR
SEASONS
SEA & LAND
MEET
N
E
S
LAND of
WILD BEASTS

STUDIO
GUARDIANS
RIDGE
GALLERY
ALLEY
ALTAR

LAND of
THE ROLLING
HILLS
DESERT'S
STONE

Prologue: The Invitation

Deep in sleep, a tone interrupted her aimless dream, the gentle note erupted from the back of her mind. The note was soft like an afterthought, like the lingering sweetness of honey left on the tongue. Gaining volume, the sound evolved with momentum. Softly, like the start of an orchestra, layers of music struck the same pitch. A complex symphony of instruments matched the key, fluttering, dancing around the note in different tones and octaves. The sound was dense, layered, and dimensional, cuing the resurrection of a nameless and beautiful vision. She felt the dynamic sounds soaking into her soul. Exhilarating her. The force of the music swelled within her dream.

Suddenly colours exploded and set ablaze like lightning over a sheet of black canvas. The colours swirled slowly and steadily across the page. Pastel blues transitioned into rich purples, fiery yellows melted into vivid reds. The tones of music synchronized as one as the strings struck the note in perfect unison. Colours stretched across the canvas, deepening and swelling, responding to the power of the music. They were one. Echoing the flow of each other, their energy was founded from the same source. From within the centre of the colourful chaos a faint glow appeared, the light brightened, expanding between space. A voice, calm, steady, and familiar broke amongst the pandemonium of sound and colour.

"Come, Annona."

Without warning, the words spoken shaped into letters and stretched themselves across the coloured sky. Across the coloured canvas they were hastily written in cursive, the ink dipped in gold.

A gushing wind blew in from the east. Visions of a valley covered in dry bones swept the colours to the sides. The colours surrounded the image like a curling wave. The plants were wilted, the bushes bore no leaves. Dirt wisped like a tunnel in the air, disappearing into the heavens. Centred in the heart of the valley was a simple home. A mother, aged like the sun, stood outside the frame of the door to her house. In the palms of the mother's hands she held a rock. Gently, softly, she placed her lips to the rock, then lifted it to the heavens as to set it free. Annona watched as the rock drifted to her. Landing at her feet, she picked it up with care, embracing the item in the same posture of the mother. A sudden wind came rushing through the valley, barrelling, sweeping the image away like chalk-dust blown from a board. The dust landed, forming a new image.

As far as she could see were rows aligned over rolling hills, a harvest bearing fruit. Placed beside the roots of the wooden giants were thousands of baskets filled with luscious fruit. The harvest was plentiful. A mound of dirt was created beside a row of vegetables. She was drawn to the mound like moths to a light. On Annona's hands and knees she dug, pushing the soil to the side, clawing the mud away with her fingers. Her hands touched something hard, she saw a wooden handle. Pushing her fingers into the earth she clutched the object. She pulled, with resistance the object came out of the darkness, revealing a small shovel in her hand.

Abruptly the hosts erupted with singing. A choir of ten-thousand voices resounded, the sound and energy lifted her to her feet, her glistening eyes searching the heavens. They harmonized to the note of the orchestra, the sound so magnificent she was brought back down to her knees. She was not kneeling in dirt, rather, the sand. Water broke against the shore, as soft as a kiss, the water touched her knees, spreading itself over the rippled sand. The hosts cried out, "Holy, holy holy!"

Even brighter they became, illuminating themselves so vigorously she had to shield her eyes. The familiar voice spoke again,

"Open your eyes."

The song halted. In mid-air, a piece of driftwood floated at her eye level. She reached forward, capturing the hallow-wood carefully into her hands, cradling it tightly against her chest.

The wood made contact to her skin, evoking the vibrant colours to return, expanding across the starry skies. The host's voices raised an octave, the colours burst into a glorious fire, the reverberating sound of the orchestra returned. The sound was omnipresent, as dense as life, moving her, pushing her, holding her. This was not merely sound, this was life itself.

Just as the melody began, it stopped, as if in mid song. Disappearing into the black, the colours faded, the canvas revealed the words "Come, Annona." The voice—the still, small voice whispered:

"Come, Annona. Come."

Part I

The Hands, the Heart, the Mind, & the Mark

You shall therefore lay up these words of mine in your heart and in your soul, and you shall bind them as a sign on your hand, and they shall be as frontlets between your eyes.

Deuteronomy 11:18

I

AWOKEN

Her lungs filled with air, a surge of electric energy charged throughout her body. The day she had been anticipating was here. She received her invitation from the Painter to the Marking ceremony so that He would reveal her life's purpose. He would stain a Mark across her chest so that she would begin the pursuit of living a meaningful life. As it was known, today was her Marking day.

Annona's room was dark as the morning dawn hung thick in the air. The moon struggled to cascade its glow through the wooden giants to illuminate her dim space. As her eyes adjusted to the dimness, she hastily threw the sheets off, untangling herself from the entrapment of her bed. The ripples of energy within her bones guided her to move quickly throughout her room in preparation for the journey.

Flicking on her bedside lamp she put her feet on the floor, stepping toward her dresser. She matched a plain black tee with blue jeans. She stood in front of the mirror as she inspected herself, satisfied with her plain outfit. Her wavy, brown hair was quickly pulled out of her face and into a loose pony-tail. Her eyes resettled on her body. Annona's closest friends often complimented the slight in her cheekbones, or the freckles that scattered like stars across her face. Her nose was short and produced a sharp tip, and her ears pushed out more than she would have preferred. She was self-conscious of her appearance, but tried to not get caught up with what she wished she looked like. Long and slender, she was slightly taller than most of her friends and family.

Looking at her reflection in the mirror, her gaze rested on her revealing eyes that could express magnitudes without speaking a single word. Eyes that would project her feelings hidden within, despite her aversion to confrontation. Today they displayed something different: hope. Today started a new era. The beginning that would launch her new life, becoming forever her before-and-after.

Until this day, Annona's life had no true north. Like a sojourner wandering aimlessly on a map, the Artist commissioned Annona to discover the hidden passions and skills buried within her hands, her heart, and her mind. Annona possessed no responsibilities that tied her down, nor any obligations demanding her attention. The Artist instructed her to live a life of discovery: to find what natural gifting and passions laid dormant within her. As she unearthed her gifting, they no longer hid behind the veil. She, like the rest of society, was told to find what gave her joy and to pursue it. Annona's sole responsibility was to explore various projects to see what her hands, her heart, and her mind gave itself naturally to, and more importantly, that could give itself in full selflessness to helping others.

Her parents taught Annona that when her hands, her heart, and her mind worked together in perfect harmony they were not three separate entities, but one: the soul. When she discussed passions and joys she learned to refer to the three parts as itself rather than themselves, because when the crowd—the beings of the Ends of the Earth—unearthed a new passion, the three entities fused together: the three became one.

She turned away from her gaze and looked around her room, trying to recall what she needed to pack in her satchel for the journey to the Studio. Her eyes focused on her desk. Within the top right drawer lay the instrumental pieces for today's ceremony. She would not forget the handcrafted box that held the sacred items. An Elder gave the chest to her several seasons ago while she crossed the Land of Heat, leading Annona to believe the box was anointed to hold the precious Relics she had gathered while journeying.

She looked at the small clock, which nested on her bedside table, knowing she needed to be at the Studio before the morning's sun broke. The journey to the Painter's Studio was a few hours walk from her village, Guardian's Ridge. She went over to her desk, and leaned over to the drawer. Annona scanned her desk, which revealed journals stacked like towers from her journeying, several writing pens, and a few textbooks about foreign tongues and cultures hazardously piled one on top of the other—the slightest wind would cause the tower to tumble.

The Artist granted each member of the crowd their unique gifting, skills, and talents. He entrusted each member of the crowd to experience their own discovery of their gifting hidden within their hands, their heart, and their mind. Until they came of age for the Marking ceremony, their undertaking was to pursue a life that was fulfilling. Enveloped in an act of selflessness, they pursued projects that came natural to them and could help others. In pursuit of their gifting, they would travel from one end of the earth to the other: the Land of Sand, the Land of Four Seasons, the Land of Water, the Land of Ice, the Land of Wild Beasts, the Land of Heat, the Land of Rolling Hills. The members of the crowd could go anywhere their feet would take them as they discovered what gave them purpose.

The life they lived before they received their Marking was a complete contrast to the life they lived afterwards. In the life of discovery, often they felt as if they were living in shades of grey: they lacked confidence in their abilities, they experienced many failures when trying new projects, and they wondered if there would ever be more to life than what they had.

In contrast, life after being Marked was like living in technicolour. Everything they experienced seemed vividly alive, overcoming failures would happen, and life burst with significance and purpose. The days of unearthing their gifts were behind them. No longer would they search for the meaning of life. Now, they wore an engraved Marking that told them and those around them precisely what they could contribute to effortlessly. With great influence, their talents would enhance the project being obtained. The Marked lives had meaning. They now confidently wore their purpose across their chest, and were able to give themselves to better their society. In return, this granted them purpose, joy, and fulfillment in life.

Annona pulled open the drawer, a loud squeak protested from the desk. A soft breath blew on the back of her neck causing the muscles to twist and squirm. Such was the sensation that overcame Annona when she saw her sacred box. It was not for what was laid before her, but for the Relics that were hidden in darkness laying within: the items she chose when discovering her passions.

She reached down, lifting the box out of the drawer, then slowly, carefully, placed it on the cleared surface of her desk. Annona traced her finger along the grains of the handmade box, the tip of her finger finding the latch. The idea of pondering over the Relics one last time sparked in her mind—reviewing them had became a habit before climbing into bed at night—but she wouldn't open the box now. She knew she needed to wait until she met with the Painter, to keep the energy stored in her, so that when the time came, the emotions would spill out of the floodgates to Him.

Taking her satchel from where it hung on the chair, she opened the bag, gently placing the box within the large pocket. She zipped the pouch to protect it from falling, pulling on the tab harder than she needed to. She scoured her room, probing for anything else that she might need. Her eyes fell upon her incomplete Masterpiece: a simple canvas hanging on the exposed wall opposite her bed.

The moment that anyone from the crowd was born, a canvas, created by the Artist, began to fill with splattered colours and hazy shapes. The Masterpiece, as it was known by the crowd, was a beautiful artwork that the Painter would define for those who lived their lives pursuing their Marking. While discovering their passions, the canvas would display new swirls of colours, yet lacking definition. After having been Marked and living a life devoted to one's calling, only then would the canvas take form and outline an image.

When the Marked exhaled their final breath on the Ends of the Earth to inhale their first breath in the land called Love Conquers All, their Masterpiece—like a legacy—was given to the Gallery. Other pieces hung at the Painter's Studio. The Marked mounted the beautiful canvas on a wall of glory alongside the countless other Masterpieces. Members of the crowd saw the lifelong painting as a testament of good work devoted to society. When they viewed the painting, it would inspire those mesmerized by the unique canvas to relentlessly pursue their own Marking as well.

The Artist created each Masterpiece as an original. No two pieces the same, the artwork always unique. Some paintings had similarities as the final image might display the same picture. But, upon further inspection the crowd noticed different strokes of the brushes and vast hues of colours used to create the piece.

As Annona had not yet been Marked, her Masterpiece lacked definition and order. Her Masterpiece possessed swirls of different colours; dark blues, royal purples, deep reds, all colours that gave her an inexplicable feeling of elation. The cluster of colours on her canvas caused her heart to shift into gratitude whenever she viewed them. Colours appeared when discovering what her hands, her heart, and her mind gave itself naturally to. Today, this would evolve. Today was the day that her Masterpiece would begin to have order, altering the colours to establish an outline and exhibit a defined illustration.

Annona wanted to remember the colours in this state: the swirls, the absence of organization, and the messiness of the piece. She scurried into the other room to snatch her sneakers. Promptly returning to her bedroom, she put them on while resting on the side of her bed, her sight going back and forth from tying her shoes to the artwork. Next time, when she would lay eyes on her Masterpiece, it would be different. With her shoes tied, she bounced to her feet, stepping in front of the incomplete canvas. Her eyes feasted on the canvas for one last time, then turning on her heels she grinned as she headed for the front door. Hurling it shut behind her, she too closed the door to her aimless existence, stepping into the wonderful abyss of the new.

2

ALLEY OF THE INVISIBLE

Many of the crowd hid from the early dawn, but within a few hours the avenues of Guardian's Ridge would hum with noise and chatter. The Marked would rise with the sun as they made their way to work that offered them meaning and purpose.

The Artist invited each member of the crowd at various seasons in their lives to the Studio, some of them even on hundreds of occasions. The crowd could determine whether they wished to undertake the invitation of the Painter. At any moment if one of the crowd had come of age and determined they wanted to receive their Marking, they would have immediate access to the Studio.

Even with the universal knowledge of the Artist, the Marking, and the Masterpiece, the crowd had a choice whether they wished to discover what their hands, their heart, and their mind gave itself naturally to. One decided if they wanted to be Marked by the Painter, and it was an independent decision for them to alone choose.

Annona walked tentatively to the centre of Guardian's Ridge, following the dimmed lamp posts that escorted her along the smooth sidewalk. Located a few blocks over from the centre of the village was a Gallery Annona attended. The Gallery hosted the Marked and the crowd who worshiped the Artist. From the time Annona was little, she had formed hundreds of memories at the Gallery, and now that she was older she preferred to walk past the building whenever she could. Recollections would rise to the surface of the conversations she had with her friends and family. She would be reminded of the discussions presented by the Shepherd.

Annona chose the quickest route to take her to the Gallery. She needed to pass through the Alley of the Invisible, a road often bypassed because of its ever-darkness and the hosts who inhabited it.

Before Annona had been born, the village named the pathway "Alley of the Invincible" because of its location between the bank and the hospital. The Gallery, known as a house of worship, stood directly behind these buildings, at the end of the Alley. Three powerhouses: finances, health, and spirituality, all within one block of each other, the heart of Guardian's Ridge. Because of this, they declared the pathway a historic street of the village.

Many rotations ago, on a chilly fall day, the village of Guardian's Ridge and the mayor met at the opening of the Alley. A ribbon-cutting ceremony inaugurated the completion of the project. The mayor of the village delivered a speech, advising the crowd of the importance of managing finances responsibly, pursuing good health, and acknowledging with reverence one's spirituality. With these three elements in balance, one would do well to stand against life's struggles. The mayor unveiled a sign that arched over the two buildings, declaring the Alley, "The Alley of the Invincible."

Absentmindedly, Engineers and Architects failed to account for the height of the two buildings. An everlasting shadow loomed over the Alley, forming an aura of endless gloom and eeriness.

The two buildings' brick walls rose so high that the sun only peaked through when it set at high noon, casting the illusion that blackened night was the sole state of the Alley. At nightfall, it was rendered pitch-black, for the stars were not visible to anyone who walked on its pathway, nor did the stars produce any light to illuminate the way. The staggering walls eclipsed the Alley all throughout the day. The sun made no difference whether it shone or the full moon casted its glow, the Alley constantly remained sunless and moonless.

Once the crowd noticed that the Alley was dark and eerie, they deserted the pathway of the Alley. Repair and maintenance frequented the main and side roads of Guardian's Ridge, but they ceased tending to the road of the Alley. Cement uprooted and became jagged, sharp rocks scattered the asphalt, and weeds ravaged the path. The hazardous path made it easy to lose one's balance and stumble.

The crowd tossed their garbage or dropped off unwanted items in the mouth of the Alley. Plastic bags floated in the dead wind like ghost-kites, and the rodents scavenged and shredded the trash across the road.

Within a week of its inauguration many of those who found themselves in harsh circumstances, the poor, or those ill relocated to the Alley of the Invincible. The Alley became a hub they could rest in without the crowd ridiculing them or chastising them to move out of their way. In turn, the crowd found the pathway even more eerie; they were apprehensive of roaming through the bowels of the maltreated. For those living in the Alley, it provided a place of refuge.

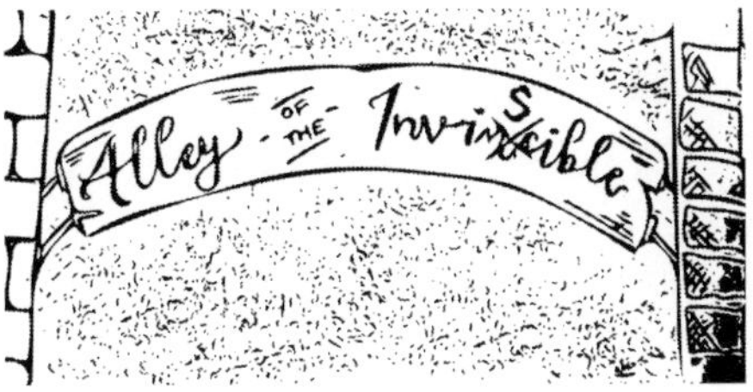

Arching Sign

In the same week of its commencement, someone vandalized the arching sign, crossing out the "nc" and replacing it with an "s", renaming the roadway "Alley of the Invisible". This new name was readily accepted as it offered a stronger truth than what it was formerly declared.

Members of the Gallery walked an extra three blocks to avoid passing through the Alley. They concluded it was safer to go around than to risk getting themselves dirty before attending the Gallery, or—and indeed worse—brushing themselves against someone who might be considered dangerous. Uneasiness grew in Annona's belly whenever she needed to pass through the Alley on her own. Her senses heightened, making her acutely aware of her surroundings.

She pulled the bag tight to her side, her knuckles whitening around the strap of her satchel. Annona ignored the warnings she had heard many times from her friends and family. She had gone through the Alley plenty of occasions, but never alone, and always during the day.

The rocks crunched as they scraped against her sneakers, cautioning her that she now walked in ungoverned territory. She viewed posters and signs that once stretched across the walls with relevancy, now torn and withered, the information now archaic and irrelevant. Barbed wire dangled from the gated windows like fallen dead branches. She glanced to the sky where the two buildings formed a narrow stream of black atmosphere. She understood she was staring into the infinite. One would expect to see the stars, but as she strained her eyes she longed for the stars to give her equilibrium, but they were not evident through the gloom.

Deviants had shattered the streetlights along the Alley while others burned out long ago. Several of the lamps flickered sporadically while the other few that survived unscathed had the bulbs stolen from them. They projected enough light through the burned glass for Annona to see a few feet in front of her.

Annona heard muffled voices from within the Alley. The reverberating sound echoed between the brick walls, striking Annona as odd that such an animated conversation was taking place at this early hour of the morning.

She stepped with caution, straining her eyes to make out the shadowy frames and figures around her. Some of the crowd slept on cardboard boxes, while others, rolled up in tarps, slept closely to each other for warmth.

The source of the sound came closer. Laughter bellowed throughout the Alley. The contagious sound of a deep belly laugh, mingled with the sound of a high-pitched hyena. Annona tried to contain her own smile as the sound rung like bells, causing those who struggled to sleep to roll over and cover their ears. She faintly recognized the laugh, but couldn't summon in that moment to whom it belonged.

Annona approached the two responsible for the commotion. As soon as she caught the outline of the shadows, she recognized it was her dear friend Adah. Adah's laugh wasn't a small laugh, but one that projected from within her belly. The Painter had Marked Adah with "Provider". Short and sturdy, her loving embrace took the wind from your lungs with just the slightest pressure from her burly arms. Dark red hair that sat at her shoulder's matched her intense personality, and bright grey eyes as brilliant as glass penetrated to the onlooker's soul.

The Shepherd of Adah's Gallery invited her to speak as she had been pursuing her Marking relentlessly the past several rotations around the sun. Beside Adah stood another of the Marked, however Annona could not read his Marking as he partially covered it with his sweater.

"Annona! What a pleasant surprise! Truly a surprise!" Adah's smile beamed as she slid her duffle bag off her shoulder and onto the ground.

"Adah, how are you?" Annona embraced Adah. Adah only came to Annona's chest, but the strength in her vice-like grasp forced the air to expel from her lungs. Adah released her as Annona looked over to the stranger again. His mismatched clothing had patches of dirt and holes scattered throughout the material. His face needed shaving and personal care. A broad gash was apparent on the back of his hand. He offered Annona a brief half-smile, his eyes promptly dropping to the ground.

Adah stepped closer to the stranger, setting a hand under his elbow. The stranger lifted his eyes to Adah, clenching his jaws together before producing a sober smile. "This is Osias. We've been friends for many rotations around the sun. I've come for him because I have found him shelter and work—"

"Just until I'm back on my feet," Osias cut in. "Then I will pursue my Marking again."

Adah nodded her head. "Yes, until you are on your own feet again." She tucked her hands into her pockets.

"That's wonderful, I hope you all the best," Annona said.

"Thanks." Osias gestured to Adah. "Adah, I'm gonna grab my pack." He pointed to the side of the Alley where a backpack rested upright on top of a mat and a rolled sleeping bag.

"Yes, grab all that you need." Adah stepped back for him to pass.

"So, Annona." Adah shuffled closer Annona, her tone much quieter than it was before, but still loud enough that anyone within several feet would overhear the exchange. Adah was the type who effortlessly gathered the crowd's attention while telling a story; the fluctuation and cadence of her voice coaxed like a song. "What are you doing in the Alley so early in the morning, and by yourself? I'm sure you've been advised to not be here alone?"

Annona was grateful in that moment that the Alley was dimly lit, if it hadn't been Adah would have seen her cheeks turn to red. "Yes, I've been told that I should stay on the main roads, but sometimes it's so inconvenient to walk the extra three blocks."

With no need to see Annona's rosy cheeks, Adah must have sensed her embarrassment. "Oh, don't worry. I always cut through, offers me a chance to catch up with my friends and to identify their needs, you know? Just—well you know how it is. Sometimes shady things can take place here."

Annona knew she was right, it would have been wiser to walk around. Nevertheless, she admired how Adah had composed herself so comfortably with those of the crowd who were in hardship.

"Do you know many who live here?"

Adah looked behind her shoulder before returning to Annona. "Yes, I probably know all of them... maybe not by name, but at least conversed with them."

"So they all have no Marking?"

Adah shook her head briskly, her hair like red ribbons flapping against her cheeks. She pressed close her eyes. "It's a common misconception—"

"No, sorry!" Annona retracted, suddenly embarrassed by her hasty judgment. "I shouldn't have assumed that just because they are here they don't have a Marking."

Adah scrunched her lips to the corner of her mouth. Annona watched as she weighed her words."It's okay. Happens all the time, you know? Yes, some have no Marking, but at least half have Markings from the Painter. But, they aren't pursuing it. They've covered it, stained it, or scratched it out. Others here have considered their Marking as inaccurate to their passions, even scribbling their own Marking on top of it! Half the battle is just helping them to see that their Marking is not what is *causing* their suffering, but can actually free them from their suffering."

"What happens to the Marked who continue to neglect it?"

"Well, of course, pursuing their own version of the Marking only lasts for a while. They try to live an ordinary life, ignoring the Marking from the Painter. But, neglecting doesn't cause the feelings to go away. Oh no, the symptoms always rise."

"The symptoms?"

Adah's sharp eyes sunk into Annona, dancing in the low light produced from the broken lampposts. "The symptoms, Annona! Anger. Bitterness. Aching. Hopelessness. Denying your Marking always causes the symptoms. Accepting a fake calling does nothing to give hope! It makes it worse, you know? And the symptoms that rose from denying their Marking pushes themselves into mental misery. Not pursuing their Marking only worsens the symptoms. Some of the Marked in this Alley—" she pointed behind Annona "—they wander around as if a crater—a black hole—is constantly causing misery within their chest, burrowing into the edges of their hearts."

Annona's breath felt trapped within in her chest, a wave of panic washed over her.

"Of course, you can't see it, only feel it. Only sense the hopelessness when they talk to you. And, you know when they have the symptoms, obviously, because they all ask the same questions."

"What questions?"

Adah leaned closer to Annona, forcing her voice to a throaty whisper. "'Is this really all there is? Isn't there more to life than this? Is my life meaningless?'"

Someone behind Adah let out a heavy cough, the hollow sound reverberating through the Alley like thunder. Adah stepped toward her duffle bag, unzipped the large compartment, and pulled out two small bottles. She spotted the source of the noise, offering the vials to the one who was coughing. The individual expressed something to Adah as they accepted the items from her hands. Adah squeezed her shoulder, returning to Annona.

"We need the Marked to pursue their Markings," Adah said, diving right back into the conversation. "Not only does it better society, it betters themselves, too. Look how the Masterpiece works! Works hand in hand with our Marking, doesn't it? The more you give yourself to your Marking, the more beautiful your Masterpiece becomes. I know of so many who deny their Marking, and their Masterpiece never reaches the potential the Painter had for it." Adah clucked her tongue against the roof of her mouth. "I'm certain it breaks His heart."

"It's never made sense to me: those who have chosen to be Marked but choose not to follow their Marking."

"I can tell you why!" Adah pushed her curly hair from her eyes. "The answer is simple: following their Marking might be what their hands, their heart, and their mind give itself naturally to, but there is a cost. Following requires surrendering their desires for the desires of the Artist."

"Yeah, that's true." Annona paused, wrestling with her answer. "But, if the Painter Himself gave it to you, how could you not pursue it?"

Adah chuckled. She looked over at Osias, standing quietly beside his bags, giving space for them to have the conversation. She kept her eyes on Osias while she spoke to Annona. "Sometimes, one of the crowd receives a Marking they believe they are not capable of, or the Marking stained on them is not true to what they desire. It's easy to conclude we know ourselves best—even better than the Artist. They assume the Marking on them is too great; the work is awfully hard, and the sacrifice requires too much. It is more pleasant to live a life based on what they deem as comfortable, which is to pursue their own version of happiness or purpose. So they give up. They don't pursue it. They pick their own thing." Adah let out a tight laugh before she proceeded. "Want to know the worst part about it all?"

"Tell me."

"What they do not realize is the happiness or purpose they experience is nothing but a weak imitation. The pure source that the Artist designed for them is the only thing that brings true hope. They carry a fictitious version of joy prone to wither away like the grass—" she threw her hands to the air "—and changes as quickly as the seasons, like the impossible task of capturing the wind."

The heaviness of the truth lowered over them like a weighty blanket. She thought of Adah's words, reflecting on the few she knew of the crowd who bore no Marking. Their lives were in endless chaos searching for purpose but powerless to obtain it. Like the futile task of trying to hold water in your hands, happiness would come for a period, but it would surely slip through the cracks and trickle away. A small cough sounded behind them. Adah stood straight, returning her focus to the Alley she stood in. A thought hit Annona: the symptoms of those who bore no Marking and the Marked who neglected it were the same.

"Now, on the other hand," Adah's voice was loud enough for all to hear, "are those who pursue their Marking. We who believe our Marking is our sole purpose even if it doesn't always feel like it. We trust the Painter knows what is best, and that He has a purpose and plan for us, no matter what we might be experiencing."

"Yes, He does." Annona pulled on the levers of her strap, tightening her bag. "You asked why I'm in the Alley? I've received my invitation to the Painter's Studio and I'm making my way there now." Instinctively

Annona flicked her wrist to align her wristwatch to the centre of her arm, checking the time. "And, I'm running late!"

"Oh, my! It's your Marking day? And here we are talking about not following your Marking!" Adah laughed again. "And you've got your Relics?"

"They're in my bag." Annona smiled.

"I actually forgot mine, you know! So excited to get to His Studio I completely forgot them at home in my bag." Adah looked off to the side, Annona sensed she was envisioning the Painter. "'Course, that was no problem for Him. Quick snap of His fingers and they appeared!" She whistled, shaking her head. "I remember my Marking day so well, as if it happened yesterday. Yet so much has changed since that time." Adah suddenly paused, her voice caught in her throat. "You know, Annona, your life is about to turn upside down."

Annona sensed the surge of excitement channel through her body.

"But, go! I've probably made you late!" Adah playfully pushed on Annona's shoulder.

"I won't be! Bye, Adah!" Annona said as she trotted out of the Alley. She peeked back to Osias, who was quietly leaning on the wall. He gave her a grin and a brief wave, Annona returned the pleasantries.

The remnants of the conversation with Adah resounded in her ears. If following your Marking meant having to sacrifice your desires for the betterment of others, then the opposite must be true of those who did not pursue their Markings. Their lives were consumed with what they could gain, filled with seeking joy only for themselves. They would do their best to accumulate whatever happiness they could find.

The crowd needed one another to find their Marking and to pursue it diligently. As the crowd pursued their Marking, an unleashing of harmony and peace flowed throughout the lands. Those in need of hope received healing. An overflowing well of love burst in the deserts of hate. There was a presence of calmness, of constant light, and no space for darkness. No gifting was better than any other. Each talent was instrumental to the harmony and progression of their village.

Annona's family wore their Markings proudly. Her mother and father modelled a life of pursuing their Markings: they invested, encouraged, and strengthened Annona and her siblings to foster what their hands, their heart, and their mind gave itself naturally to. Annona could never imagine living her life ignoring the Artist and being Markless.

As she left the Alley, the surface of the ground changed from broken gravel to cobblestone. Dozens of streetlights lit up the roads, providing visibility of the buildings and structures around her. Annona sensed the gentle whisper of a breeze on her face. She paused, turning her head to the right side of the street where the Gallery stood in all of its grandeur.

3

THE GALLERY & THE ARTIST

Before her stood the Gallery, meticulously cared for and not one element of the building out of place. Members of the Gallery purchased and applied new paint, signs, and shrubbery after the change of four seasons. They believed keeping the Gallery fresh and modern would help to attract the crowd who did not attend the Gallery. The contrast of the Alley and the Gallery would forever taunt with Annona's opinion of justice and greed.

Massively constructed, the Gallery could receive five thousand from the crowd. The architectural design of the building was state-of-the art. Staff of the Gallery loaded it with the most modern and innovative music and sound equipment. In the heart of the structure stood an oversized hall, able to host elegant galas and the events of the most famous and well known among the crowd.

The Gallery in all its grandeur

Annona attended the same Gallery for as long as she could recall. Even though the contrast of the Alley and the Gallery caused a pit of unease in her stomach, she had some of her best memories in the Gallery. A place of worship and adoration for the Artist, the space provided her with stability. She also established some of her greatest friendships there. At the best of times, the community of the Gallery became like a family to Annona.

As she made her way past the Gallery and several other buildings, she passed another Gallery on the other side of the street. Behind that Gallery, two opposing Shepherds placed additional houses of worship within the same block. On the other end of her village and scattered throughout were nine other Galleries.

Why there needed to be thirteen Galleries in Guardian's Ridge seemed perplexing to Annona. The population of her village was hardly three thousand. Her place of talks and adoration alone could host the entire village and more. However, there were some that did not recognize every belief that the one Marked Shepherd had, thus they set up their own Gallery. The "new" Gallery would reinforce their own interpretation of the holy book, known as the Book of Suneidésis.

Annona carried herself along the path, loosening and tightening the straps on her satchel as she marched. Wedged between a loose rock and the cement of the sidewalk was a pamphlet from the previous week's gathering at the Gallery. Annona swooped down to pick it up, inspecting the paper from front to back. The pamphlet provided a space for the crowd to take notes on the talks given by the Shepherd. On this pamphlet someone had filled the note section with a messy scrawl. Annona read the title of the talk, called "Who is the Artist?"Annona scanned the pamphlet, remembering how the talk gave Annona a deeper love for the Artist and His compassion.

The Shepherd focused the last gathering at the Gallery on the character of the Sculptor, the Potter, and the Painter. Annona strained her eyes to decipher the note under the dimmed light.

The Sculptor created all, everything seen and unseen. Known as many names to the crowd, names that often speak of protection, creativity, power, and provision. He is strong, the one you call on in times of distress; He is kind, generous with mercy and grace; He is selfless, prepared to do whatever it takes to abolish the void between you and Him.

He is known as the Sculptor (His name from Guardian's Ridge) because of His ability to give life. He sculpted the mountains, carved the wooden giants, crafted rivers, gave form to animals, and ignited breath to everything manifested from dust. His visual appearance is unknown to most, but He riddled whispers and hints of His glory throughout all creation.

The Sculptor knows the Marking that each member of the crowd will receive before it is revealed to them. This is because He is the one who creates them, choosing every detail for them: their gifts, talents, affinities, passions, abilities, limitations, and dreams.

The Potter is the son of the Sculptor. He is the reconciler between creation and the Creator. As there are some in the crowd who do not pursue their Marking, chaos and suffering are produced in the ends of the earth. The Potter, of His own accord, acted as the restorer between the broken vessel of creation. He has all the same attributes as His Father, the Sculptor, but His form looks like one of the crowd. The Potter, like His Father, is immeasurably compassionate. This is His distinguishing trait that captivates the Marked, establishing in them an unquenchable yearning to experience Him. The Potter's heart breaks for those who are in infliction or pain and He loves profoundly for those who feel shame, remorse, or have given up. Because of the Sculptor's heart of wanting no separation between Himself and the crowd, the

Potter laid down His life so that He could eradicate the division between the crowd and Himself, providing direct access to the Sculptor.

The Potter advocates for the members of the crowd to pursue their Marking diligently because of the good it radiates to all when they live their lives selflessly—

Annona flipped the pamphlet to the backside as her eyes searched for the top of the page to continue reading of the last character: the Painter.

The Painter is the breath of the Sculptor and the Potter, released and commissioned by them to reside in the ends of the earth and amongst the Marked. He is the voice of wisdom dislodging the confusion, the steady anchor within the stormy seas, and the flood of water bursting forth in the desert. He gives inspiration and determination to the gifting and passions, sanctifying them for their Masterpieces.

When the crowd receives their Marking, it is the Painter who unveils the Marking to them, through the wisdom of the Sculptor and Potter.

Everything they do is consistent, in flawless unison, never contradicting one another. When one expresses their blessing, it is as equivalent as being blessed by the three. They are three names attached to one substance; we can interchangeably use the name of the Artist as the Sculptor, the Potter, or the Painter.

Annona dropped the note to her side, her eyes pensively searching amongst the shadows of the buildings and the surrounding mountains. She did not believe in coincidences, only in providence. She concluded that the Artist had appointed this pamphlet where to settle so that Annona would stumble upon it.

Annona had experienced these moments of larger-than-life coincidences before. She's had the unexpected financial gift dropped in her bank account when she was nearing the red; a sudden opportunity to pursue a gifting when the positions were already filled—moments of pure wonder. It was in these moments in which the physical and the spiritual realm collided, and in the midst she stood, marvelled and speechless.

Her eyes swept over the notes again, re-reading the characters of the Sculptor, the Potter, and the Painter. A wave of goosebumps spread from her arms to her head. The words from her dream resounded within her mind, sending a second wave of goosebumps from her head to her neck.

"Come, Annona. Come."

4

MEMORIES OF FAILURES & DISTRACTIONS

She took the note and folded it in half, then in half again. She pressed along the crease, opening the flap of her satchel to store it in the outer pocket.

Annona returned her gaze to the circling ridges. The shadow of the summits covering the village were a few hues lighter than the night sky. Her eyes followed their path until she saw the faintest glow of a light halfway up the mountain. The light indicated the site of the Painter's Studio. His Studio rested on the side of the cliff, like a nest perched on the top of a wooden giant. The local crowd named the place the "Eagle's Perch". From anywhere in the village you could see His dwelling place, a beautiful physical expression that the Potter was amongst the Marked.

The Painter had Studios in every village, in every land, all across The Ends of the Earth. He was omnipresent, like the wind, able to be everywhere at once. When the crowds from different villages received their invitation to the Painter's Studio, they would travel to the one that was closest to their village.

Annona had the urge to run to the Studio, but she did not want to arrive too early. The excitement within her was ready to burst. She anticipated the meeting for so long. Annona had prepared what she wanted to tell the Painter; desiring to share with Him the Relics she had found that gave her joy. She wanted to describe to Him the colours that appeared on her Masterpiece, and although she could not offer the perfect words as to what the Relics meant to her, she believed He would be able to do so.

Annona made her way to the path that led to Eagle's Perch. As she walked along, recollections of all the journeys she completed throughout her life kept bubbling to the surface. She reminisced of the hundreds of hours she dedicated to uncovering what her hands, her heart, and her mind gave itself naturally to.

As the good memories emerged, simultaneously it trudged up the memories of her mistakes and failures that she had experienced. She recounted the myriad of disappointments when attempting something new and failing. She had been powerless to give her hands, her heart, and her mind as she wished they would be able to.

Annona sought to help others using medicine, only to recognize that her mind could not embrace the complexities of the biology of the body. She attempted to draft new laws with politicians, but found her heart wrestling to study thousands of regulations. She struggled to work with engines, connecting tubes to belts and radiators. Her hands were clumsy, unfit to achieve what the hands of other's could do so naturally.

Annona found tasks that her hands and her heart could give themselves naturally to—like music—but her mind was unwilling to remain devoted to practicing the instrument or to create a piece of music that was original.

When passions like medicine, laws, engines, and music failed, it did not derail Annona. Although she knew she found interest in the various projects, she was not truly passionate about the work nor saw the skills as instrumental to her future.

Physically she was walking to the Painter's Studio, but her mind continued to reminisce of when she went to the Land of Wild Beasts, encountering her enemies for the very first time. To recall her failures meant ruminating through the memories of her enemies as well. As she kept her eyes focused on the trail, she reflected on her first experience with the Masters of Failure and Distraction.

She had been resting on a bench outside the classroom; her head sunk into her hands as she went through emotions of frustration and despair. Another lesson in a foreign tongue, and again Annona felt like she had learned nothing. She had left her village in pursuit of finding a new Relic, determined that language would be one of them. But, it wasn't. Language would not come to her naturally even though she had tried. So, there she sat, resting on a bench, wallowing in pity. A sloshing sound emerged from down the hallway, slipping and sliding along the ceramic floor. The sound was sporadic, like a fish flopping against a dock, squirming for air. Annona directed her eyes to the noise, the culprit slugging its way to her.

"How can you expect to help the crowd in an unfamiliar land if you cannot learn to speak a new tongue? Something so simple; yet, you stumble and choke on your own words!" Its discharge of words spewed out of its gaping mouth as it struggled to catch its breath.

The creature was short and bulky. Its height only came to Annona's shoulders and yet it weighed four times as much as her. From the top of its head it oozed a thick concoction of black tar, the consistency like molasses being poured from a bottomless jar. The tar seeped, dripping off its fingertips and toes leaving a sticky trail behind it, and leaving a shallow puddle around the creature whenever it stood still. The tar excreted from every surface on its body, masking any distinguishing characteristics of its face or form.

Annona tilted her head back, sickened and taken aback by its appearance. "Who are you?" Her nose crinkled as she caught an odour of musty sweat.

"I am Kachash, the Master of Failure." Kachash coughed uncontrollably. The cough mutated into choking and hacking; small balls of grey spit rocketed from its gaping mouth, exposing yellowed and browned teeth.

"Ka—what?"

The creature waved a finger as thick as a sausage in the air, spitting out the last of its hacking.

"Kachash. Ka"—it dropped its jaw, over enunciating the vowel—"*chash*, you know, rhymes with trash." Annona tried to hide her curling lip, she watched Kachash struggle as she slid herself away from it on the bench.

Tar concealed Kachash's skin, leaving a mystery to what laid beneath. The consistency of the tar-like-liquid reflected light, like scales on a fish. Like warm glue left out on a sunny day, the mixture appeared sticky. Its body was covered with scraps of debris, accumulating forgotten fragments of the earth: dead branches, leaves, dirt, and garbage stuck to it like a molasses covered flytrap. Kachash splattered its tar on anyone who remained within its path, and if they stood with Kachash long enough, they found themselves covered in its sludge. Feelings of failure and despair spread from the infected areas to the rest of their body, attacking their heart and mind.

Kachash tormented Annona, convincing her that even after collecting her Relics, the Painter would give her a Marking that was meaningless.

"Your efforts of discovering your passions are worthless. The Painter will never finish your Masterpiece, and everything you do will result in failure."

A smudge of the dark syrup trickled down Annona's knee, while several other drops splattered onto her forearm. Annona shook as she wiped the tar from her leg, smearing the colour from cement black to a coffee-stained brown as it thinned across her skin.

"Oh, look at you, you poor thing!"

Annona jerked her head around, her attention gripped by the soothing, velvet voice. From the opposite end of the hall came another creature, and unlike Kachash, this being was charming and well kept, displaying itself with a sense of grandeur. It glided towards her. Its head held proud as Annona had to tilt her head back to meet its eyes. Its tone was soothing and when it spoke its words were pleasant, sounding like a gentle lullaby, delighting the ears of whoever was in earshot.

"You've been trying so hard, and still you struggle. You must be so disheartened, darling!"

I have been trying hard. Annona became in tune with her tense body, her spine and arms hunched like a cat startled by a dog. Kachash had provoked her to squirm and stiffen, but this new being soothed and calmed her, allowing her mind to unwind after Kachash's cruel remarks. The scorch of her failure eased, like water to a fire. Its distinctiveness, in contrast of Kachash, enchanted her. It was a sight for sore eyes.

"How impolite of me, I have neglected to present myself. I am Perispaó, the Master of Distraction." Grimacing from ear to ear it gave a deep bow and a sharp flick of the wrist as it curled its lips, its peering eyes never leaving Annona.

Perispaó would find one of the crowd who would welcome its soothing song, rubbing their back as it chanted words of relief, and massaging the place in their shoulders that always seemed tangled in knots. It even enticed them into sitting so it could rub their tired feet, all the while singing its lullabies of distractions. It always had a million ideas of projects, activities, or distractions for the Marked to try. Perispaó was crafty as it persistently found ideas to encourage the distressed to self-soothe. This tactic allowed the Marked to take their minds off of the work they pursued, and helped ease the pain when a project failed.

The most striking feature was its eyes; piercing blue, they were like a mirage in the desert, a disillusioned pool of chilling waters that the victim hopelessly fell into, only to reveal an ambush of quick-sand and wrath. Its eyes hypnotized its victim, drawing them in. Perispaó's words were not meaningless blabber, but as it spoke it did so with such authority, to the tired mind it sounded like truth when it fell on their mesmerized ears.

Perispaó was quite ingenious, and quite the trickster. Whatever it had the Marked and the crowd distracted with was simply meaningless. The only joy it would bring was a perishable fix that kept them content for a while and did nothing in the progression of their Masterpiece. Perispaó ruled many of the Marked who were burned out, and possessed full authority over those who had no Marking and were in relentless pursuit of happiness.

Kachash and Perispaó had mastered a banter used to attack their victims; Kachash bullied them into admitting their failure, while Perispaó soothed them and urged them into a project of distraction, softening the pain of their defeat and Kachash's sharp blows.

Back and forth they taunted, with Annona paralyzed in the middle, struggling to make sense of the predicament she was in.

"You traveled far, sacrificed time with your family, and gave up the comforts of home. You must be so miserable," Perispaó said, its voice as smooth as velvet. Without permission it rubbed Annona's neck, massaging the knot Annona had developed at the top of her spine.

Kachash sneered, plucking off a fragment of a rotting stick. "You were so convinced that studying a foreign tongue would come easy to you, something that your hands, your heart, and your mind would give itself naturally to!" Kachash said, a splatter of tar splashed onto Annona's torso. "Instead, your mind operates like a stone barrier, you cannot absorb the concepts!"

Kachash was right. She needed her mind to act as a deep well, storing the words and the structure of the unfamiliar dialect in her memory. All too often her mind drew blanks when trying to recite the phrases she had just learned, causing her to stumble and twist her words.

Kachash flicked the fragmented stick from its fingers, the stick spun in the air like a helicopter's propeller and smacked against the wall with an abrupt halt. "You think that you can help the crowd in a foreign land across The Ends of the Earth, but you cannot even find the words you would require to communicate with them." Its ooze sloshed onto Annona as it shifted its feet, lifting strands of the syrup puddle that accumulated under its mass. "You are not as significant as you believe yourself to be."

Annona believed that Kachash was right—she knew it would be tough to help the crowd if she could only speak in her native tongue. Some of its tar splattered onto her arm, she swatted at the syrup, trying to rub it off as more splashed onto her legs.

Perispaó released the top of her neck, setting its hands on her drooping shoulders, kneading them, causing her to relax further into its spell. "Perhaps you should rest and return home. You've worked hard, you deserve it." It caressed her shoulders even harder.

Annona's feet had been stuck in a sticky puddle of Kachash's tar, while her mind played Perispaó's lullaby on repeat.

I worked hard. I tried my best. I deserve a break. She glanced over Kachash and Perispaó once more, both gave her a convincing grin. In that moment she made up her mind to return to Gaurdian's Ridge for a few weeks. With her mind charmed by Perispaó's spell, she crammed her suitcases with her belongings and wallowed back to her village.

Annona had journeyed halfway back to her home before she realized they had enticed and deceived her. Shame filled her. She had forgotten the Artist's truths, how had she been able to so easily abandon His truth? Even more humiliating—how had she not seen their attacks as a trap? Nor used the Potter to unveil the lies?

With a repenting heart, Annona spoke with the Artist. His grace surrounded and restored her, prompting her to continue her pursuit of the Relics. Annona changed course to discover a new land to reveal her joys and passions. She determined to not let the failure of learning a new tongue overcome her, vowing to speak with the Artist before making prompt decisions.

Her encounter with the Masters of Failure and Distraction took place long ago, and a lot happened since the last time Kachash and Perispaó had attacked her. She concluded they did not stand a chance of fooling her if they were to meet her now. Now, she trusted with everything in her she *would* be capable of living out her Marking, *whatever* it may be.

A chirping bird sang its morning song as Annona marched along the trail of the towering wooden giants. She picked up her pace as the sun would break through shortly. Walking along her breathing heightened as she accelerated her speed. Her beating heart matched the surge of energy as it thumped like a drum against her rib cage. The trail had begun to elevate in height. Carefully she climbed up the rocks, continuing the ascension to the Studio before her.

5

THE STUDIO

Annona had been so absorbed by her memories of Kachash and Perispaó that she did not notice the sky peaking through the leaves, changing from midnight black to a colour that reminded her of the ocean's vast blue. The beginning of daylight was upon her, the stars fading as the sun approached from the horizon, preparing to make its majestic appearance through the peaks of the mountains.

Wooden giants surrounded the stone trail as a distinct pathway laid out in front of her. The ease of the route allowed Annona to wander back and forth between recollections of the past and excitement for what the day ahead would hold.

A snap from a twig redirected Annona's concentration to find the source of the sound, her eyes straining to catch a blackened figure sharply making its way around the wooden giants. Upon first sight, Annona immediately knew who it was.

This being did not mirror one of the crowd, but looked like a ball of live electric wires. Its name was Angō. The strands that made up Angō, all chaotically rolled in a vertical angle, sticking out every which way, sparks and charges flying from the ends of the snipped tips. Using its cables it would attach itself to Annona's feet and place its wired hands on her head, inducing her to experience a distorted vision, in which she was no longer capable of seeing clearly. She would shake, feel her mouth go dry, and her mind would race to rapid thoughts of fears and anxieties, to the stresses beyond her control.

Annona assumed that Angō would find her while traveling to the Studio as it appeared to Annona more regularly than Kachash and Perispaó would.

Angō glared at Annona. "I understand you're traveling to the Painter's Studio." Angō jolted itself closer to her while sparks flew. "I will come with you." Without waiting for Annona's consent Angō put its cables on top of her feet and set its wired hands on her head.

Annona's sight blurred immediately; the visions of her failures surged to the forefront of her mind. "Does the Painter know what my Marking should be? How does He know what I desire?" The doubt propelled her into a state of panic, being so certain several minutes ago, now anxiety riddled her entire body. She stopped walking and faced Angō as it clutched on her, merely inches from her face.

Angō continued, sneering, "Perhaps it is best if you make the Marking yourself, you already know what gives you joy. Don't you know what your hands, your heart, and your mind give itself naturally to? Why not use your gifts for good and still have everything you want? Who knows you better than you?" Angō tightened its constraint on her head.

"You could be right, maybe the Painter will give me a Marking that won't make me happy—that will demand too much of me."

Annona's heart pounded to a strange pulse, beads of sweat dotted on her forehead. The butterflies fluttering inside her stomach morphed into bats, trembling and smashing one into the other. Her feet seemed like lead, as if someone had fastened weights to them. She lowered her eyes to her arms, noticing a slight scar on her palm.

When Annona first set out to uncover what her hands, her heart, and her mind gave itself naturally to, a group of farmers had offered her an opportunity to work the land. She used a trowel to turn the earth, to give the soft dirt hidden underneath layers of hard soil a chance to emerge. While she dug in the mud the trowel hit a rock, causing her hand to slip and graze on the blade. The accident was so sudden that Annona didn't react in time to pull her hand away. The ragged metal scrapped against her soft skin, causing a gash to open on the palm of her hand. Small beads of blood appeared, the farmer working alongside her helped to wrap the wound in a bandage. Initially the cut stung, but the sting quickly vanished as she felt more preoccupied with the work she was accomplishing and the purpose she discovered in it. She preferred using her hands to work, this was one of the joys that she found when she was journeying: a passion that she would share with the Painter. She wanted to use her strength to work the earth, it was something that her hands, her heart, and her mind gave itself naturally to.

This sudden eruption of memory shook Annona, ordering her to wake up. She realized she had allowed Angō to set its wired hands and cables on her, submitting her calmness to its static being, exchanging her tranquil mind for its anxious concerns.

"Off! Take your hands off me, I depend on the Artist!" Annona cried, pushing away Angō as she stumbled to free its restraint from her. Angō extracted its wires from her head and broke loose from her feet. Annona's vision instantly returned and cleared.

Angō slouched down, its form shrinking to less than half of its original size. Annona stepped aside as it wandered back down the path from which it had appeared, prowling in the seclusion of the wooden giant's shadows. Annona focused her eyes forward, back onto the path to the Painter's Studio, which was now only a few minutes away.

As Annona shifted her thoughts from anxiousness to anticipation, the gravel transitioned into a flat passage, leading her directly to the entrance of the Studio.

The Studio looked like a conservatory with many windows and minimal walls. Large stones stood erect, providing skeletal support between the glass surfaces. The stones felt perfectly smooth to the touch; they were the type of rock only formed in a shallow river, exquisitely polished from the endless water rushing over it.

When she came to the entrance of the Studio, she saw that there was no door. Instead, two massive beams were set upright, planted several feet apart from each other. The two beams stood supporting a third, which served as the framework of a doorway, resembling an arbour. Glass walls surrounded it. She approached the frame, running her hands over the smoothness of the wood, recognizing a carpenter must have devoted hours to sanding it, producing a glossy polish to the touch.

Annona peaked inside. "Hello?" Her voice ricocheted off the hollow walls.

"Child, please come in!"

She heard His voice before she saw Him. The tone of His voice reverberated through the hallway, rich and tender.

"I'm around back!" His voice came from an unseen room.

Annona stepped into the Studio. The walls of the short hallway were astonishingly high, using no lights to illuminate the space, as the natural light gleamed through the glass arched ceiling, revealing the emerging sun peaking through the ridges.

Annona's mind had to catch up with what her eyes were witnessing. Displayed before her were thousands of paintings, each individually framed, and mounted on the walls. The illustrations were beautiful and overwhelmingly peaceful. She realized she was standing in the presence of the great legacies of the Marked, who devoted their entire lives—blood, sweat, failures, triumphs, strongholds, and victories—to completing their canvas: Annona was surrounded by the Masterpieces.

Walking through the hallway, Annona was taken aback by the thousands of Masterpieces. As she indulged on the illustrations staged on the wall, something drew her attention to a canvas depicting the impression of a magnificent sunset slipping behind purple and grey mountains. The huge wooden giants were covering the surface of the summit and helped to portray the illusion of the series of never-ending mountains.

She took in the image, amazed by the attention to detail. It appeared as if a gentle breeze were swaying the wooden giants, causing them to swing rhythmically with the reddening sunset. Annona stepped closer to the canvas, realizing it wasn't an illusion of wind, rather the strokes of paint were actually moving. The whites, yellows, and oranges that were chaotically but methodically painted in horizontal and vertical strokes began to vibrate and shift in direction. As she gazed more intensely into the image, it altered its movement and colours altogether. Greens, blues, and purples overtook the softer hues, generating the order of the strokes to relocate to a different spot on the canvas. While the colours rearranged, the outline and the illustration of the image remained the same, constantly projecting the same picture.

Masterpiece in the Hallway

"I love that piece." The Painter moved closer to the piece, head tilted back as His eyes traced along each corner. "It's one of my favourites."

Annona turned to see the Painter standing in the hallway, leaning on the frame of a doorway. His dishevelled hair had specks of colours in it, and paint had been splashed all over His clothing. He wore a brown apron to remove the excess paint from His brush, accomplishing little to protect His shirt and jeans against the mediums.

"It's fascinating," replied Annona, her focus returning to the piece. "It's changing colours and direction."

The Painter smiled. "That's something I cherish about my Masterpieces, they're constantly evolving, making it easy to find favouritism in them all."

Annona took a step towards the paintings and gazed more intently at the multiple pieces. He was right, each piece was alive with movement. The colours shifted gradually, flowing and swimming across the canvas as if a spoon stirred the colours, like heavy cream added to black coffee.

Annona had seen Masterpieces before, as they had several framed canvases hanging in the atrium and the sanctuary of the Gallery. But the Gallery had only twenty, at the most twenty-five completed pieces. She admired the Masterpieces in the Gallery hundreds of times before, but had never witnessed the paint moving. Making a mental note, she would check the pieces the next time she was in the Gallery.

A low, rumbling sound erupted, Annona felt the floor beneath her feet shake. Out of the corner of Annona's eye she detected something on the floor moving. New wall space ascended from the floor, raising the paintings and the ceiling even higher, providing more area for the Masterpieces to be displayed.

The Painter observed Annona with a gentle smile, allowing her a minute to take it all in. He planted His hands in His pockets and spun on His heel, heading back to the room He appeared from. Annona glanced once more at the Masterpiece that had captivated her. Dots of purple now appeared in the centre, establishing a new sun. Sighing with wonder, she followed the Painter and entered the room.

6

TOKENS & TRANSFIGURATION

"What would you like Annona, coffee... tea?" The Painter strode to the kitchenette stationed beside the door. He reached for the kettle below the stone counter, placed it in the sink, and filled it with flowing water from the faucet. He kept His back to her as He grabbed mugs and spoons from the cabinets above. Annona redirected her attention from Him, taking in the beautiful domed conservatory they were standing in.

Tokens & the fire pit

An exceedingly grand, round-shaped, stone fire pit centred the room. The walls of the pit came knee high, and roughly two hands wide. Balanced in the form of a teepee, the firewood was placed in the centre, ready to be lit. Arranged on either side of the pit were two worn, wooden pews. Scattered on top of them were several red weaved pillows and plush blankets, creating a cozy seating area. He had arranged a few pastries and fresh fruit on a slate of rock. A large chuppah staked around the fire pit and pews; fresh flowers, vines, and eucalyptus covered every inch of the pillars. A piece of white, silky fabric spread over top of the chuppah, forming a canopy.

The floors were composed of concrete and rock, but had been sanded and smoothed to create a flat, even surface. The room bore the frame of a glass sphere, windows covering the dome shaped ceiling. From the grand windows one could make out Guardian's Ridge below, resting at the base of the mountain, vague lights appeared as the early risers of the crowd woke in the village below. A view of the wooden giants surrounded the Studio, and the splendid sky was in the premature stages of sunrise.

Surrounding the conservatory was a massive, low standing bookshelf which created a seamless, level surface, abutting the windows. Custom built by the Artist Himself, the bookshelf was deep and wide, capable of holding thousands of books. As the room was circular, He built the shelves to make sure that there were no gaps between them, but instead the shelves looked like one perfect ledge, outlining the entire room.

Starting after the kitchenette, they followed the circumference of the room, and finished at the door they entered in. On the tops of the bookshelves were thousands of items, too many for her to count.

These items were the tools used for every industry imaginable. Not made of its normal material, they had been produced with elements of rare metals and rocks. Tungsten and titanium, gold and silver, silks and parchments, the items glistened like stained glass windows in the morning hue.

On the tops of the book shelves closest to her were musical instruments. A violin made of gold, built a fraction of its normal size, was the first instrument she saw. The creator constructed the strings with black steel. Engraved around and through the base of the instrument were swirls of decorations. Nestled beside the golden violin was a set of drum sticks, created out of a rich mahogany, the signature of the musician inscribed on the side of the sticks. A microphone had been decorated with diamonds, rows of the rock sparkled in the morning light. Annona saw multiple instruments lined behind, but the bookshelf next to it stole her attention. It had the tool's of a surgeon: medical instruments, stethoscopes, thermometers, and tweezers. Like the instruments, the tools had been created out of rare elements. She picked up a stethoscope, made from topaz and quartz. She inspected the diaphragm of the stethoscope, rubbing her thumb against the flush quartz. On the next shelf top were carpenters tools. Several hammers, some created from tungsten, others from titanium, were set vertically on a rack. A rack beside the hammers held screwdrivers, saws, and nails, majority of the tools made with darker materials. Beside the carpenter's tools lay blueprints, some rolled and set in piles, others stacked on top of one another, revealing the raw images of hundreds of famous structures. He had covered one shelf with maps, compasses, binoculars, and notebooks. Annona flipped through a black leather-bound notebook. Inside were notes and names of places from the ends of the earth, and the recounts of a Captain's travel.

Next to the discovery instruments were chef's knives made from gold and silver, bronze spatulas, and rolling pins created from pine. A mosaic tiled box was filled with recipe cards in alphabetical order, the secrets to thousands of mouthwatering and prized dishes filed within. Another shelf had running shoes created from leather, water bottles made from glass, and stop watches crafted in silver. There were clipboards, full of strategies and plays that teams had used to seal their victory. The shelf beside the athletic equipment had technologies old and new, sketches of inventions, circuits, lightbulbs, panels, and wires. Beside that shelf were cameras, films, and flashes. Stacked were thousands of beautiful pictures, some in black and white while others were saturated with colour. On the same shelf stored paint brushes, oil crayons, sketch pencils, drawing pads, pencil sharpeners, clay, and a potter's wheel sitting on the floor. Similar to the other items, the artist's tools were created from rare rocks and metals.

An invisible force drew Annona to a shelf that had server's aprons, name tags, and notepads. She flipped through one of the engraved notepads, reading the server's notes: *extra ice, the child's name is Tikva, ask about her sick sister*. The notebook was full of details like this, alongside their food order. A shelf overlaid brooms, buckets, and cloths, the supplies required to make something look beautiful and to return it back to its initial grandeur.

"Annona?" The Painter repeated, His voice the same tone as He peaked over the miniature refrigerator. "Would you like coffee or tea?"

"Sorry! These items are beautiful. I'll have a coffee, please." Annona walked from shelf to shelf, as if at an art venue, captivated by the vendor's pieces.

One piece begged her attention: a globe, smooth and textured to the touch. Whoever designed the globe created the borders of the land by using gold foil, inducing the globe to glisten in the morning light. A steady and experienced hand had written in flowing typography, labelling the names of the land. The detail of the globe was astounding: rivers, deserts, rain forests, mountains... it was all precisely and meticulously arranged.

"Ah, yes, that truly is a wonderful piece." The Painter approached her, passing Annona a mug filled with piping hot coffee. The mug was a hand-thrown potter's creation, a one-of-a-kind speckled with cobalts, dark greens, and blues. Surely the mug was beautiful enough to be shown on display like the rest of the items, but the Painter insisted she drink from it.

The vast volume of the Painter's instruments amazed Annona. "How have you compiled these items?" Annona asked. "These beautiful items, the unlimited quantity," her voice trailed off as she paused, thinking. "They must come from every End of the Earth." The artistry and uniqueness of the pieces took her aback, as she had only made her way through a third of the shelves.

"Yes, you're right. I received them as gifts, all from the Marked sincerely pursuing their Marking." The Painter picked up a framed portrait, the image was one of the Marked, given the Marking "Mother." In the photograph the Mother was smiling from ear to ear as she carried a small baby in her arms. The Painter's smile stretched across His face as He viewed the image. "Expressions of their gratefulness." He carefully returned the picture to the counter.

The Painter took a long draw from His mug, turned, and faced Annona. She looked past the Painter, longing to see every item on the shelves. He let out a small cough, grinning at Annona. When He smiled His entire face smiled with Him. "Are you surprised by My appearance?" the Painter asked, keeping the mug below His lips.

Annona, for the first time, truly set her eyes upon Him. The features of his face were smooth, His skin covered in freckles. He had a scruffy beard and a pointed nose. Green eyes, the colour of dark pine needles, were cornered with crow's feet. His smile encompassed the source of warmth, a small gap protruded between his two front teeth. He kept His wild brown hair tucked behind His ears. He wore a pair of faded and torn jeans, a white v-neck that needed washing due to the splatters of paint that covered it, and a pair of black sneakers. The Painter's apron was brown, weathered: speckled with paint and plastered with strokes from paint brushes.

Annona nibbled on the inside of her lip, pondering the question while observing His appearance. His eyebrows raised, sending rows of wrinkles to emerge on His forehead as His eyes danced with playfulness.

"Your form has always been a mystery. I've heard from some of the Marked who describe You as a creature that possesses four hooves, while others have suggested You resemble a living thing that has paws. Another told me You look like smoke, so thick and white it is impossible to see through." Annona took a small sip from the mug. He had brewed the coffee to perfection, tasting notes of dark cocoa and spiced fruit, and the warmth of the brew was not too hot nor too cold. The coffee's taste was delicious. She hastily took a second and third mouthful, keen to consume the coffee as fast as she could.

The Painter's grin grew to a broad smile. He raised His mug to His lips and flipped His head back to polish off His drink while lifting His hand to Annona motioning her to pause.

Reaching out with His free hand He asked to take her mug. The Painter took the mug from her, reaching over Annona to rest both of the coffees on the shelf of items behind her.

He slid back several steps from her, placing Himself near the centre of the room, as He inspected His arms and legs. He returned His gaze to Annona, searching her eyes as He rested His opened arms at His sides. Ambitiously, He filled His lungs with oxygen, drawing in air as if He was about to jump into a pool of water.

The second His mouth closed, the form of His body withered away as a gust of wind wrapped around Him. His hair floated like a plant underwater. As the wind grew stronger, the Painter's skin softened and cracked into flakes. It changed from the texture of skin, softening into specks of fine particles, floating in the air. The dust floated around Him, until His body was no longer evident, expanding like swirling sand across the desert. The dust lifted as if instructed by a conductor to move. It took the shape of a cylinder—a rotating column of air—the dust wrapping around itself continually until it paused in unison, then suddenly transitioned into drops of rain. The head of the cylinder bubbled and stretched, evolving itself into a magnificent cumulonimbus cloud. Bolts of lighting flashed from within the veil and stuck sporadically throughout the surface of the mass. Crashes of thunder reverberated throughout the hollow dome while the melody of rain pelleted like rocks thrown to the floor. The rain did not expel itself across the floor as it naturally would, instead it showed restraint by staying directly under the thunderstorm. As soon as the pellets of water touched the floor they would disappear, somehow being absorbed into the stone ground. The storm lasted for several seconds. The fury and magnificence left Annona awestruck. Abruptly, without warning, it paused mid strike: the cloud and rain became perfectly still. It slowly rotated in place so that Annona could see the tempest from every perspective.

As soon as the storm completed rotation, the mass collapsed in on itself causing the storm to shrink smaller and smaller. Like a black-hole, a suction of air in the depths of the magnificent cumulonimbus cloud absorbed the pellets of rain, the lightning flashing relentlessly in the bowels of the vapour. Annona felt a tug on her clothing, her hair whipping against her face. She positioned her feet, setting herself against the undertow. The cloud retreated inward until it was a fraction of its original size, confining itself into a glassy marble that levitated in midair.

The clear marble floated at Annona's eye level. It drifted towards her, pausing at arm's length. Annona stared intensely into the marble, inside the transparent ball was the eye of the storm: the fury of the elements roaring within.

With the sound of a thundering crash, the marble exploded into a million pieces, spraying the tiny shards all over the room. Annona's arms raised to shield her face, but when the fragments hit her body, she wasn't cut, nor did she feel pain. The shards felt like sprinkled droplets of ice-cold water. Annona peaked from behind her shielding arms, glancing at the specks on her. They illuminated like stars as the specks shone all over her body, giving her an angelic glow. She touched the glowing droplets with the tip of her finger; it was like gel to the touch. She rubbed the gel between her thumb and finger, releasing an aroma like the scent of the earth after a downpour of rain. The perfume intensified as it lofted across the room.

The illumination of the droplets became more powerful, brightening themselves so greatly that she once again protected her eyes from the intensity, but it did little to stop her from seeing the glow even behind her shielded eyes.

Like a light switched off in a dark room, the glow behind Annona's closed eyelids ceased. She slowly opened her eyes. In front of her stood a pillar of smoke ten feet high, so dense that she couldn't see through it. The cloud smouldered and expanded, but remained in perfect control spreading itself across the room.

Annona looked to the floor at the base of the smoke, expecting to see a heat source that was creating such a thick pillar of smoke, but there was no fire, no such source to generate the thick vapour.

Just as it started, the smouldering transitioned into a swirling motion. It churned upon itself, rotating and weaving, as the vapour transformed into particles of dust, and the dust formed the outline of a body. From the chaos, arms, legs, torso, hands, and a head formed. As the body assembled, the dust changed into skin, until every speck was back in order, and before her stood the Painter; His head bowed, and arms opened to His sides, ending exactly as He had begun. He raised His head and exhaled, deeply, calmly.

Annona stood, dumbfounded as to what she had just witnessed. The Painter stepped towards her, as He brushed His hair from His forehead, His voice emulating calmness.

"I am what the Marked need Me to be. I am the coolness of the wind on a sun scorched day; the life-giving liquid in the rain to quench plants; the shine of the stars on the blackest of nights; the winding stream that bursts forth in the barren deserts. I am the Answer, the Guide, the Still, Small Voice that speaks truth to you in times of uncertainty, and the Peace that descends upon the afflicted mind. I am the Compass. I am the

North Star. I am the seasoned Captain that knows his way out of the storm," the Painter said, smiling, as He stepped closer to Annona. "To speak to Me is to speak to the Sculptor and the Potter. I am Them and They are Me. I am the breath you exhale, and They are the breath you inhale."

The Painter reached for her hands, lifting them while gently opening her clasped grip, His hand tucked under hers. Inside her palm was an illuminated droplet. It sparkled, shining so brightly it caused a glare. The Painter extended His finger, took the droplet onto the tip of His finger, and spread it across her forehead.

He looked at her forehead with satisfaction, giving a quick squeeze to her hands as He released them and stepped pass her.

Annona realized she had been holding her breath. She released it slowly, envisioning the tempest in her mind—the remnants of the echos of thunder rumbling within her ears.

7

GOLD & FIRE

The Painter reached behind Annona and took her half finished drink. He walked to the kitchenette, filled the mugs to the brim with coffee from the dripper, and strolled back to her while balancing both mugs in hand, one from the mouth of the mug and the other by the handle. Annona watched the Painter with wonder as she took the mug from Him and sipped the coffee. The coffee tasted as if it had just finished brewing.

When she drew the mug from her lips, her hand slipped, causing the hand-thrown mug to fall, smashing itself into several pieces on the floor.

Annona gasped, jumping back from the shards of the jagged mug scattered on the concrete. Her eyes jerked to the Painter, His head tilted as He was looking at the broken fragments of the mug.

"I am so sorry! It slipped from my hands! I can be so clumsy." Annona hastily threw herself to the floor, frantically picking up the broken pieces of pottery. The Painter knelt down beside her, setting His hand on top of hers.

"Allow Me," He said, His tone filled with kindness. He took the pieces from her hands and collected the others that remained tossed on the floor, like shells scattered along the sea.

"Don't feel embarrassed, mistakes happen." He chuckled. Annona met His eyes this time. His demeanour remained soft.

He carefully collected each piece, delicately placing the shards in the palm of His hand. As they were kneeling on the floor together, He reached into the front pocket of His apron and pulled out a small container. Hardly able to hold two small coins, the vessel rested in the palm of His hand. A dulled silver, the container was scuffed and layered in scratches.

The Painter twisted the lid, revealing a gold like liquid inside. Freeing His right hand, and with great tenderness, He dipped His finger into the solution. He then traced His fingers around the jagged edges of the pottery, making sure that the gold serum covered each area of brokenness. Like a master of puzzles, He inspected the rugged shapes, attaching the damaged pieces to where they fit perfectly. The gold liquid was like glue. He was recovering the mug back to its former figure, but now there was a layer of gold between the cracks, giving the mug even more beauty than it possessed before.

With great satisfaction He looked over His work as He passed the mug back to Annona. "See, it is more beautiful than before."

The smell of the spilled coffee lofted to her nose. He glanced at her, knowing that she wished to clean the splattered liquid from the floor. "Let the spilled coffee be, the smell pleases Me." The Painter deeply inhaled, His head tilting back and shoulders tightened together as He smiled. Twisting the lid back on the container and returning the vessel to His pocket, He slowly released His breath.

Mug Restored with Gold

Annona inspected the mug, the contrast of the cobalts against the gold was extraordinary. When she readjusted the mug in her hand to peer inside, the coffee had been filled to its brim. She tilted her head in confusion, how had the coffee been replaced in her mug? The Painter avoided her eyes, a teasing smile stretched across His face.

The Painter stood up, taking His coffee back into His hands. Annona noticed His speckled hands covered in paint, mainly hues of oranges and yellows. She followed along His painted hands to His arms, past His shoulders and rested her gaze on His kind smile. He looked into her eyes, setting His hand on her shoulder.

Annona experienced a sensation that was like warm water being poured on her head; the invisible liquid trickled past her shoulders, down to her legs, and ran along her feet. She looked to the floor to see the substance, but the ground was dry, showing no sign of the water.

The Painter smiled, His voice soft as He spoke, "Today is your Marking day, Annona. The day you understand what your hands, your heart, and your mind give itself naturally to. I know that you have traveled to The Ends of the Earth, and I recognize that you have tried hundreds, indeed thousands of tasks trying to discover what you can give yourself to. Along the way you have experienced pain. You sensed disappointment when passions did not prevail, and Kachash and Perispaó entered your life. Other intruders visited you often. I know that Angō made itself known to you as well. You have doubted whether the struggle has been worth it, and there have been many times you've been alone."

Tears formed in the corner of His eyes, but His hands on her shoulders remained steadfast, they did not lose their grip.

"Today, we declare and reclaim hope over the places inhabited by despair. We acknowledge that through hardships, trials, and pain, character is produced, and Annona—there is good character in you." The corners of His mouth raised to make a smile. He squeezed her shoulder and motioned her to sit on the wooden pew by the fire pit.

Annona walked beside the Painter to the bench, under the chuppah. The sweet scent of the white roses and eucalyptus delighted her. She saw how they intertwined with the wood of the pillar, the white roses in perfect bloom. The Painter sat down beside her, taking another draw from His mug. He relocated the tray of fruits and pastries behind Him. Annona gazed at the pit, the fire was not yet started, and she knew the flames were instrumental in receiving her Marking.

She glanced at the Painter. "Would you like me to start the fire?" She nodded her head in the direction of the pit while drawing the dark fluid to her lips.

The Painter forcefully swallowed His mouthful of coffee, gently shaking His head from side to side while He kept His focus on the pit. "No, it's okay," He said. "I'll make the fire."

When Annona returned her gaze back to the pit, the fire ignited from the centre of the teepee, the smoke and sparks swirling towards the fabric of the chuppah. An uncontrollable smile grew on her face while she shook her head in wonder. The Painter chuckled as He raised His eyebrows a second time, returning the mug to His lips for another sip.

Annona watched the trail of smoke raise from the fire, a cloud forming under the chuppah. The silky material draped across the arbour allowing the smoke to pile underneath it. It filled until it could hold no more, the smoke spilled out and raised to the glass roof. Annona leaned back on the pew, beyond the fabric of the chuppah to examine the glass roof. The ceiling was constructed without a chimney, nor did it have any type of structure for the smoke to escape through, yet the room did not fill or smell of smoke. It simply disappeared as soon as it touched the glass, evaporating at contact with the surface. She traced her eyes back to the cloud under the chuppah, the vapour swirling and twisting like liquid smoke.

"This is My fire, Annona. My fire only purifies. It is not like the fire you are familiar with, which gives warmth and can burn." The Painter set His mug down on the pew. He picked at the dried specks of paint on His hands, rubbing them as little bits fell to the floor. The Painter put His hands to His knees, lifting Himself to His feet. He walked over to the stone wall of the pit, placing Himself closer to the flames. He observed the dancing fire for a few seconds, crouching down beside the pit. He hesitated for a moment; His focus intent on His hands. Swiftly He placed His hands deep into the belly of the fire, the flames stirred and roared while the sparks swarmed like lightning bugs.

"Painter!" Annona jumped to her feet and threw her hands to her head. The Painter kept His hands in the fire, rubbing them against each other as if He was washing them. Looking at her, He smiled. She released her breath, realizing He must know what He was doing. He kept them in the belly of the fire for several seconds, gradually pulling them out. He held them like a surgeon after scrubbing in to operate, then lowered them to Annona's eye level, allowing her to inspect them. His hands were not harmed, not a single burn was on them. All the paint had been removed—His hands were impeccably clean. No specks or blemishes remained; the flames obliterated the stains.

"My fire only purifies, Annona. My fire renews whatever is willingly offered to the flames, both the good and bad, and reconciles it to what it was first called to be. By drawing out the impurities and abolishing the mistakes, it restores it to what I designed it to be. The flames reverse the things that went wrong redirecting them for My good. Purified. Cleaned. New."

The Painter continued to show Annona His hands, rotating them from front to back. Annona studied His hands, satisfied there were no burns and astonished by how perfect they appeared. Annona observed her own hands, taking in the many blemishes.

"All in good time," He said, chuckling. He motioned for her to sit back down.

"I know that you have brought your Relics from journeying, each with a hidden expression of great meaning to you." The Painter acknowledged as He sat back down on the bench. He leaned to the floor and took His mug. "Will you show them to me?"

Thump, thump.

She felt her heart respond to His question before the words drifted from her lips.

"Yes."

8

THE LAMENT OF THE ARTWORK & THE PAINTER

Annona grinned, nodding her head as she reached for her satchel. She pulled out the wooden box that held her precious Relics, swivelling herself as she sat down beside the Painter, and gave a small cough to clear her throat.

"Does the box hold your Relics?" He asked.

"Yes."

"How did you determine what to choose for your Relics?"

Annona paused, thinking of the question before responding. "Well, choosing my Relics was relatively easy, that is, *after* I got the hang of it. At first, the 'how' of choosing a Relic intimidated me. When I was told that I had to pick an item only when I unveiled what my hands, my heart, and my mind gave itself naturally to, that seemed difficult to me."

"Why was that?"

"I had never experienced the three entities fusing to one before. I've heard about it from the Marked, Elders, and Shepherds. But I'd never experienced my hands, my heart, and my mind working simultaneously as one. I had gifts where I used my hands and my heart, or my mind and my heart individually, but never the three together."

The Painter smiled. "It can be tricky to determine when the three are working as one, but choosing the Relics is not meant to be a process that is hard."

"No, and it wasn't, but for me it didn't happen very often."

"And the times that it did?"

Annona couldn't help but smile. "As soon as I experienced my hands, my heart, and my mind working together seamlessly for others, it was as evident as black ink on a white canvas. I felt like pain did not seem to exist and hope would have the final say. I experienced moments when every ounce of flesh and every cell within my body burst alive, overcome by a perfect peace."

The Painter's entire body nodded in agreement.

"The experience was rare when it happened, but I sensed a radiating joy unleashing within me because I was giving myself to something greater than my own selfish desires."

"Yes, that's exactly what you needed to experience. What else did it feel like?"

Annona looked at her hands. "Within my being I felt my hands, my heart, and my mind fusing into the soul."

The Painter's eyes twinkled with delight. "So in those moments, you chose a Relic?"

"Yes," Annona said. "Only in those sacred, extraordinary moments, I would choose an item that would symbolize the inexpressible joy I experienced."

"Your Relic," the Painter said, "will prompt that inexplicable emotion that stirred in you as you were using your hands, your heart, and your mind seamlessly, and that same Relic will be significant in the revealing of your Marking."

Annona nodded in agreement, her hand tracing along her box.

"How many have you chosen?"

"Three," she said, her hand suddenly pausing on the latch. "Wait, is that enough?"

The Painter scratched His nose with His free hand. "Members of the crowd can collect as many Relics as they want. There is no too little Relics nor too many chosen. Nor is it important exactly what the Relic is, as long as the Relic reminds you of the feeling you encountered to unleash the deeper meaning experienced."

Annona thought of her Relics. She chose Relics from diverse lands: she discovered the first Relic at a farm in the Land of Four Seasons, another outside a hut in the Land of Heat, and unearthed the final Relic on the shore of the Sea and Land Meets.

"Yes, with these three Relics, I'm ready."

"Good," He said. "Let's begin."

The Painter shifted in the pew to get Himself comfortable and Annona did the same. She clicked opened the latch, lifted the lid, and placed it gently behind her on the bench. She traced over the three Relics, her fingers settling on the one she preferred to start with, taking the Relic into her hands. The Painter waved His hand as He lowered His head, giving her the freedom to start.

"To uncover what my hands, my heart, and my mind gave itself naturally to did not come quickly for me. I often experienced work that seemed meaningless and mundane rather than projects that were meaningful. I encountered many failed attempts at discovering my passions—sometimes wondering if any of it was worth it." Annona hesitated, unsure if she should express what laid heavy on her heart. For quite some time, she had questions for Him that danced along the borders of accusations. The questions felt like boulders that had invaded her heart, weighing her down. She glanced at the Painter as He waited, shifting Himself closer to her.

"You can share with me the ugly, Annona. I know it is there. No need to hide what I already see." Unfolding His arm across the back of the pew, His fingers stretched across the pine, grazing against Annona's shoulder. He tucked in a knee, His foot placed under His bent leg. His body was now aligned to hers as He tilted His head slightly down. His mug remained in His left hand.

Annona nodded. "Painter..." her voice cracked, she coughed, looking at her hands. "Telaah and Peirasmos visited me repeatedly, appearing more frequently to me than many others of the crowd I know."

Her mind's eye pictured the Brothers: Telaah and Peirasmos. The Brothers were the Masters of Chaos and Suffering. The suffering that these two brought with them was of a profound nature—not one that could be easily endured. Instead, it was an inescapable journey of trauma that the crowd fought to persevere through. Their evil tidings could bear any type of suffering: the death of a friend; sickness of a family member; revelation that the workers you aligned with were wolves in sheep's clothing; even the confession that your dearest friend and ally was rallying against you, plotting your demise.

Telaah and Peirasmos were twins: inseparable, identical in appearance, and cruel. They came whenever and to whomever, as often as they were ordered, bringing terrible news. Small in stature, the tops of their heads hardly touched the bottom of Annona's knees. Telaah and Peirasmos, if not for their height, could have been mistaken for one of the crowd.

Using their shortness and weight as a weapon against their victims, they delivered tragic news. Telaah would cling to the victim's back, attaching itself like a leech, bearing down with its heftiness. The other Brother, Peirasmos, would grab the victim's leg, making each step weighted, strenuous, and painful. For some, this suffering could last for seasons, until the Brothers would dismiss themselves—finally detaching from the victim's back and legs.

Annona's voice heightened as she continued. "The Brothers did not attach themselves to me once, or twice, or even three times..." Annona paused, her words caught in her throat. "I've met some of the crowd that have not even met the Brothers yet. When friends, family, or the Marked hear how often they visit me, they insist I must be doing something wrong." Annona's voice cracked, the Painter's eyes remained trained on her. "Telaah and Peirasmos were at the door to my home more times than I could count. They invaded my home, being so accustomed as they were to being sent to me, they invited themselves to my dinners and rested themselves in my bed. At times when there should have been only joy, I could not release myself to happiness because of the weight they inflicted upon me." Annona's eyes filled with bitter tears. "They attached themselves, their weight pressed deep into my shoulders as they unleashed news of conflict and pain. They've disclosed the ulterior motives of my closest friends, exposing my fear that I am alone. They robbed me of joy and confused my understanding of my relationship with the Artist. When the Marked saw how often they came to me, they would say 'everything happens for a reason,' dismissing my suffering." Annona paused, dropping her head. She whispered the words that came to her lips, needing to confess them to someone, "there were moments when I gave up."

The Painter nodded His head, continuing to look at Annona, His face filled with compassion. "Annona, do you believe I ordered the Brothers to be sent to you?" He asked with the volume of His voice slightly above a whisper, the sound of the crackling fire a trifle louder than His words.

Annona thought about the question. It was the relentless, loaded question she had asked herself many times before, only uncovering the truth while in the midst of her hardship. She searched around the conservatory, the items on the shelves sparkled like white sand along the beach. Shadows danced around the room, cast from the wooden giants towering outside the glass dome.

Taking a moment she found her voice and spoke with certainty, "Initially, yes I did. I thought I disappointed You. I assumed You were trying to teach me a lesson. I thought You had abandoned me. I was *so* angry with You." She tightened her grip around the Relic, shifting in her seat. Her eyes darted to His face, afraid that He might deliver judgment—but, He showed none. What she found instead was pain.

"But then?"

Annona's grip around the Relic loosened. "But then, I learned they had no 'sender'; their source of chaos and suffering was fuelled from those of the crowd who were not following the Artist. I saw that anytime I cried out to You, You had not abandoned me." The tension in the Painter's face softened. "Sometimes, You came when I called out to You. Your presence came all around me and Your perfect peace flowed through me. Other times the Marked encouraged me, emphasizing *who* You are and the good You have accomplished in me. But, what I experienced the most was silence. I learned that in the quietness, still You were with me. You always found a way to remind me that You are for me, with me, and have me."

The Painter set the mug beside Annona's box, reached over, and took Annona's empty hand. "Always. I have always been with you, and I always will be with you: through the pains of suffering and into the moments of immense joy," the Painter's voice was kind and soft as He squeezed her hand. "I know that in moments when you were discovering what your hands, your heart, and your mind give itself naturally to, the Brothers visited you. Yet still, you found your Relics when you were surrounded with suffering. You've shown that even through the sorrow, you will choose to follow your Marking." His hand slipped away and wrapped around His mug once more.

Encouraged, Annona's heart was lighter, as if He removed the barriers that calcified onto her heart. She lifted the first Relic to show it to the Painter, her voice more confident than before.

9

ROCK, TROWEL, & DRIFTWOOD

"This is my first Relic: a rock I took while in The Land of Heat. We spent several weeks building a home for a mother who had lost her husband. We put the finishing touches on the home, painting the walls of the house green. The sun was hot. There were children dancing, singing, and playing all around us. I remember the time had came to give her the keys to the door, completing the project. We surrounded her as we poured out blessings over her and her new home, and I remember looking at her expression when we told her that the house was hers, ready for her to move in. She didn't smile, rather, she wept... she had no words. I myself don't know which words I could use to describe seeing her in that moment, but I felt honoured to be part of the project in providing her with shelter." Annona rubbed the smooth side of the rock with her thumb, placing the rock on the bench in the space between her and the Painter.

The Painter smiled from ear to ear. He picked up the rock, tracing the smooth surface. "She was at a loss for words in that moment, but her heart told Me she felt honoured, too." He set the rock down, smiling at Annona.

Annona picked up the next Relic: a small gardening trowel. "I used this trowel a long time ago, on a farm in the Land of Four Seasons. We turned the earth so we could plant small seeds. I can still remember the fragrance of the wet mud, the warmth of the sun on my back, and visualize the hard dirt turn into soft. I was on my knees and could feel the hard soil surrounding me. When I would dig the holes and place the seed inside, I could envision the plant bursting forth in the next season and the fruit it would produce. I enjoyed digging and planting, but it was another degree of emotion when I was asked to help pluck the ripe fruit in a field ready to be harvested. I did not grow tired of reaping, knowing that the work I performed would benefit hundreds of the crowd, feeding their stomachs—giving them the nutrients needed to live," Annona said, passing the trowel to the Painter.

The Painter picked up the trowel and looked it over. "I remember hearing your words as you were thanking Me. I remember the gratefulness thick on the lyrics of the songs you sang," The Painter said as He looked at Annona. "I'm delighted you've chosen this Relic." He placed the trowel beside the rock, carefully lining the two side by side.

Annona smiled, reminiscing on that sacred moment. She placed her fingers on the final Relic, closed her eyes, and searched her mind to find the words to begin the tale.

"There was a time—a brief time—when I visited Sea and Land Meet, near Gaurdian's Ridge." Annona kept her eyes closed, envisioning the images that needed to be spoken in words. "I escaped to the waters to find refuge and rest, as my home no longer was a refuge. The Brothers refused to leave me; they were crushing down on my spirit. Angō's wired hands were latched on me, making my vision blurry in the night. I couldn't fall asleep. Perispaó was there as well, relentlessly insisting that I distract myself with a new project and Kachash's tar had stained my skin. My journeys had been difficult. I came to my home to find rest, and yet it had been invaded with the Masters. I could trust no one and

I was alone. It was in the dead of night and I was restless, eager to find peace. I realized my only chance of obtaining peace was by seeking You. I searched for refuge where the Sea and Land Meet, near my village. When I arrived I was met with an inexplicable sense of peace filling the air. You had come for me. I took off my shoes; I was standing on holy ground. I could sense You in the breeze and I could see You in the splendor of the night sky."

The Painter smiled at her, taking another sip of His coffee.

"I stepped onto the sand. Walked towards the water. Dipped my toes into the tide. The water was warm, the sky was clear, and millions of stars shone above me. Angō had withdrawn from me, Perispaó released my shoulders, and Kachash was nowhere to be found. The Brothers had relinquished for a few minutes, allowing me to be alone with my true thoughts. Painter, do You remember what I told You that night?"

The Painter's eyes welled with tears, His lips quivering, as He reached again for Annona's hand. "Artist, I will go wherever You send me. I will love whoever You put in front of me. I will give to them whatever You need of me." The Painter paused, a tear fell, trailing down His cheek. The Painter nodded as He whispered, "Your servant is willing. Use my hands, my heart, and my mind. Send me."

Annona's looked at Him through tears. "Those words were the cry of my heart, Painter. That's how You know they were true. After I said those words, a fire lit in my chest, a renewal of energy burst through my bones. I acknowledged, even though I could not see You, that You had restored me."

Annona allowed the tears to flow. She had not spoken about that moment to anyone—it had grown into a sacred memory for her. The tears continued to fall as she lifted the final Relic, a piece of driftwood she had found washed up on the shore right after she had experienced the restoration of her mind and body.

"I know I was not unearthing a passion nor discovering my gifting while at the place where The Sea and Land Meet, but I had to bring a Relic from that divine moment. The declaration of my heart's cry and the restoration that was poured over me was such a strong response. I could not ignore it," Annona said, offering the final Relic to Him.

Annona's Relics

The Painter took the wood into His hands. "I couldn't agree more." He arranged the Relic beside the other two, each piece perfectly laid beside the other. "Annona, you have chosen your Relics; you wandered from The Ends of the Earth to find your passions. Be as it may, the Brothers visited you, Angō attacked you, Kachash tormented you, and Perispaó hypnotized you... yet still, you determined the will to pursue your passions and discover what your hands, your heart, and your mind give itself naturally to—and more importantly—you did so with selfless ambition." The Painter collected the Relics: the rock, the trowel, and the driftwood.

Annona smiled. *It's happening*, she thought to herself. Her journeying, the suffering, the discoveries, the joys, the highs and lows: it all surmounted to this. She watched as the Painter's smile—within half a second—transitioned into a flat line. His thumb tapped on the driftwood, His gaze searching Annona's.

He took a sharp breath in. Exhaled slowly. "Before we begin, Annona, you need to know something," The Painter's voice was gentle. Annona shifted in her seat, the muscles in her face tightening. Doubt rose in her mind. *What have I said wrong?*

10

THE COST OF THE MARKING

The Painter searched her eyes. "You *have* been visited by the Brothers often. They caused great disappointment, confusion, and chaos in your life. I know that the other beings of destruction have made themselves familiar to you, making your journey much more difficult, causing you to question your faith in Me, and even leaving you panicked in moments of terrible distress." The Painter focused on the driftwood. Annona recognized He was determining which words to use.

"You must know even after you receive your Marking and even when the image is being defined on your Masterpiece, they will continue to come. Even in following your Marking, you cannot escape their attacks. It intensifies their appetite to harm you; they will camouflage themselves from you so they can attack when you least expect it. They become more insidious as they strategize to tear you down, and they concoct new methods to cause suffering. Some you have yet to meet! They're waiting for you to be Marked!"

The Painter stood up, stepping closer to Annona. He bent down to the ground, one knee on the floor, the other perched against the pew. His shoulders square to Annona's, He set the Relics on the bench, this time taking both of her hands into His. His head was just below hers. She could see every detail in His face. As He searched her eyes, Annona was amazed by the darkened green colour that appeared bottomless, gazing back at her.

"They will try to imitate Me. They will use a voice that resembles Mine, and they may even use some of the same phrases, twisting them to confuse the truth. They will say they know Me, operate as if they serve Me, and propose that you do shameful acts you would have turned from in the past." The Painter took a deep breath. He allowed His words to submerge into Annona's mind.

Annona was looking at the Painter's hands as she tucked her hands in His, noting how small they looked inside His firm grasp. She spoke, barely a whisper, "Where will You be?"

The Painter lifted her hands, then rested them flat over her heart, not needing to use words. He gave her time to wrestle through the warning He gave her.

Annona lifted her eyes to the Painter, "As I said..." her voice grew stronger, "Artist, I will go wherever You send me. I will love whoever You put in front of me. I will give to them whatever You need of me. Your servant is willing. Send me."

With that the Painter beamed. He lifted His hands from hers and placed them on either side of her face. "I will send you!" He exclaimed with joy. "Now, let's discover your Marking."

The Painter turned Himself towards the fire, stood up, and carefully gathered the three Relics into His grasp. Taking the rock, he drew in air then breathed onto the Relic. He repeated this with the trowel and the driftwood, breathing on each Relic. Swiftly, He stepped to the pit and stacked them side by side in the belly of the fire.

The flames changed colours quicker than one could see. Hundreds of shades of blues, pinks, purples, greens, yellows, and reds flashed before her eyes. Colours that Annona's eyes had not seen before swirled and sparkled as they floated their way to the ceiling. She stared into the pit, first with caution, then with growing excitement. The sparks rose high as the smoke lifted and condensed. The smoke under the chuppah flashed rainbows of colours, swirling and shifting like a liquid. A fragrance lofted in the air: vanilla and brown sugar, some of Annona's favourite scents.

The Painter stood back as He watched. Annona admired the Painter. She smiled with anticipation as she watched Him. To Annona's astonishment, when she returned her eyes to the fire it had extinguished. As soon as it had begun it stopped; so abruptly it was as if someone had drained a barrel of water onto it. Remaining inside the stone pit were the ashes and coals of her beloved Relics, not even the logs remained. The abruptness alarmed Annona, she feared something went wrong.

"Just a few more seconds," He said as His eyes twinkled. He crouched down beside the pit. "Come closer."

He gestured for Annona to sit on the smooth surface of the stone wall that surrounded the fire pit, placing herself under the chuppah. Annona sat down cautiously, expecting heat to be radiating from its centre. Instead she felt the coolness of the rock. As she settled herself by the coals, the scents of the eucalyptus and white roses attached to the pillars reached her nose, offering notes of sweetness. The contrast of the smoke reminded her of the times she slept under the stars, sprawled out beside an open fire.

Annona's heart beat quicker as she watched the Painter govern over the coals. She studied the coals glowing all shades of red and orange—the whites fading to black.

The Painter sat down next to her. With His hands He reached into the deepest part of the ashes, and took out a large handful of the glowing coals.

"With the ashes of the Relics, which held great significance to you, the Artist reveals your Marking." In one swift movement, He wiped the ashes from the right side of her chest to her left. He put His hands back into the pit, picked up another handful, and spread them across her chest again.

There was a sensation of hot and cold, fire and ice, jagged and smooth each time He spread the ashes across her chest.

She watched as he plunged His hands back into the ashes a third and final time, sifting the ashes and coals from hand to hand, then brushing them across her darkened chest.

The Painter stood up and offered His hands to Annona, helping her to her feet. Annona stood, her chest tingling.

"Are you ready?" He beamed, wiping His hands on the side of His apron.

"You know I am!" Her mind raced with what the Marking could be.

The Painter opened His mouth, took in a bellyful of air, and blew His breath onto the stained skin. The dust scattered from her chest, revealing one, single word, engraved in black across her chest.

Harvester.

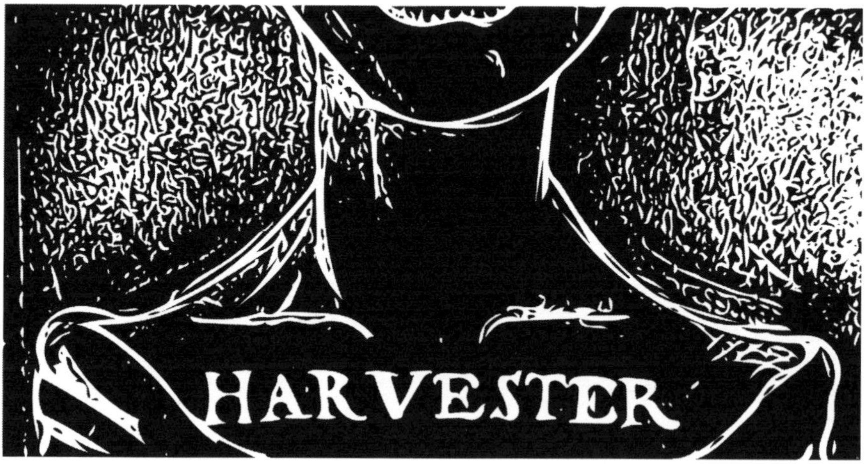

Annona's Marking etched in her chest

Part II

The Beauty of the Harvest

"But God has so composed the body, giving greater honour to the part that lacked it, that there may be no division in the body, but that the members may have the same care for one another. If one member suffers, all suffer together; if one member is honoured, all rejoice together. Now you are the body of Christ and individually members of it."

1 Corinthians 12:25-27

11

THE STORM & THE SONG

Annona plopped down on the slanted stool, reaching for her laces she loosened the knots on her boots: the laces crusted to the arch and the sides stained from mud. She kicked the boot off her heel, propelling it a few feet forward twirling in the air, as it splattered dirt on the tiled floor. Well worn from the harvest, her boots had survived into the fourth season of wear in the Land of Rolling Hills.

She stripped off her jacket, sprinkled with drops of rain and torn in the sleeve from the snags of twigs and sticks. The Season of Tears came to her village, the dry mud now being replenished each evening by the sky's waters, giving resurrection to the soil. Winds brought in the heavenly clouds, opening them to let the roaring vapours pour out their watery blessing. Rain drops the size of marbles crashed against the land while lightning lit up the dark skies. During the day, the clouds carried the elements within, allowing the sun to warm the land. But, like clockwork, the rains poured as the hiding sun set behind the thunderous clouds, granting the dry plants, the thirsty beasts of the land, and the local crowd the water they sought after.

Annona kicked off the other boot, sending it toppling beside the first. Annona stood, cracking her back and neck as she stretched her arms above her head. The storm grumbled forward like a slow wave rhythmically crashing and breaking along the shore.

Annona grinned as she collected the boots and stacked them by the entrance to her modest home. The rain started as a trickle, all the while gaining momentum. The wind picked up its pace as the thunder echoed the energy. A flash of lighting lit up the dim room. She snapped her head to the window only to see a second flash of lightning send shadows against her cream coloured kitchen.

Intrigue had drawn Annona to the Land of Rolling Hills like metal to a magnet. Other lands on the Ends of the Earth existed where she could have gone to harvest, but her intuition compelled her to this land.

The Ends of the Earth had passed four and a half rotations around the sun since Annona's Marking ceremony. Since that time, she had pursued her Marking with reckless abandon, leaving behind everything she knew. It had overjoyed her on that sacred day to receive the Marking of "Harvester". The calling the Painter gave her was true to what her hands, her heart, and her mind truly gave itself naturally to.

Within a brief time of receiving her Marking, she had left the Land of Four Seasons and came to the Land of Rolling Hills, which she now claimed as her home.

Even with the Marking and knowing her desire to come to the Land of Rolling Hills, she had faced many challenges. To start over meant leaving behind her comforts, friends, and family. The culture of the Land of Rolling Hills was not one that Annona was accustomed to; it took time for her to adapt.

For Annona, harvesting in the Land of Rolling Hills required a black and white decision. She was compelled to harvest, because she believed the Artist anointed her to be in this unfamiliar land stricken with poverty.

Life presented Annona with plenty of opportunities that were black and white. A vivid memory surfaced from when she was a child: new to a school her eyes rested on a classmate being isolated and teased. Annona dropped the toy she had been playing with, marched herself over to him, and took him by the hand—half dragging him—back to where she played. She passed him the toy to play together, not wanting him to be alone. Annona made choices to align herself with the light even if it meant she might be the only one standing in it.

In the past, situations beyond her control had subjected her to choices that seemed grey, having no clear answer. In these moments of haze and uncertainty, Annona had learned to trust her gut: the place in her body where her heart and her mind fused together; where her feelings and logic meshed as one, guiding her to know what she had to do.

But, knowing where to begin her harvest was not one of those situations of grey. Annona did not need to rely on her gut to know where to start, she knew of her calling to harvest in the Land of Rolling Hills.

How did she know? This intuition linked back to her Relic—the rock—from the Land of Heat. As she uncovered her passion for serving, all while discovering the charm of observing another culture, the experience had broadened her horizon. Perhaps due to her age, the experience in The Land of Heat had shattered her walls of innocence and naivety. The exposure to another culture laden with poverty and oppression changed her. It was as if her neurons rewired and lit up in places they hadn't before. The experience shaped the way she understood life and rewrote the trajectory of her dreams.

To Annona, the Land of Rolling Hills had been a place of influence since she was young. The Gallery often invited Elders (those who dedicated their lives to their Marking), from the Land of Rolling Hills to speak to the audience about their work, their Marking, and their Masterpiece.

The Land of Rolling Hills was a land oppressed by a political power choked by corruption, which forced the crowd to endure unthinkable poverty. It was a nation desperate for aid. While discovering what her hands, her heart, and her mind gave itself naturally to, Annona was not offered an opportunity to go to the Land of Rolling Hills. The Land of Heat had been the closest culture to the Land of Rolling Hills that she experienced while journeying. But, now that the Painter had Marked her with Harvester, she was ready to venture to the land of her dreams.

Annona turned on the faucet in her kitchen, running her hands under the stream. The water took a minute to reach a warm temperature, but it never became hot. She had become accustomed to the chilly waters. Lathering the soap between her fingers, she scrubbed her nails against her palm, trying to loosen the dirt layered underneath them.

She turned the faucet counter-clockwise; the stream slowed its force to a gentle drip. Annona flicked her hands over the sink, the droplets of water splattered against the tub.

Her stomach grumbled, reminding her it was time to prepare dinner. To save on time and resources, Annona tried to arrange the same meals on the evenings when she worked. She had learned how to make traditional dishes from the locals. The meals were high in nutrients and did not need many ingredients, which allowed Annona to buy food in the markets and to cook without much thought.

While wandering the village's markets one evening, she had found an old radio that streamed stations from every land. She purchased the radio, determined to find a station from the Land of Four Seasons. Within a few hours she discovered a station that streamed from Guardian's Ridge.

Annona approached the radio as she dried her hands with the towel, adjusting the volume so it played loud enough to masquerade the crashing symbols of thunder.

It took time, but after a few rotations around the sun and the support from her new friends, along with that of her family back in the Land of Four Seasons, she was able to adapt to her new lifestyle.

When Annona had decided that she would leave Guardian's Ridge and move to the Land of Rolling Hills, many of her friends, even some of her family, came to her with their concerns. They warned her of the dangers she might face: isolation from her community, language barriers, and the cultural differences that would exist. They advised her of the hostility and isolation foreigners experience, especially when trying to adapt to a different culture. But, their greatest argument was the little knowledge and experience she had in the Marking she was pursuing, questioning her ability to bear any fruit.

Annona did not have reasonable answers for their questions, because their questions presented no room for the Artist to accomplish what He constantly does—to cover, fill, and overflow all she lacked. All the whys did not matter to Annona. She believed in her Marking as a Harvester, and knew He would take care of the rest. Next to receiving her Marking, she was more confident in this than anything else in her life.

For every ten in the crowd that had doubted her, there was one who encouraged her, confirming her Marking and reminding her to follow her Marking.

Annona stirred the vegetables and meat together, the smell of sizzling food lofting throughout her tiny kitchen. She turned the burner down to low so that the food would continue to marinate together while she settled the lid on top of the pan.

With Annona's focus on cooking dinner, the storm rumbled past Annona's neighbourhood and made its course to another section of her village, called Desert's Stone. The radio played tracks that Annona used to listen to in Guardian's Ridge. The music transported her back to memories of the Gallery and the special moments she experienced when discovering what her hands, her heart, and her mind gave itself naturally to.

Annona returned to the pan, lifting the lid to check on her food. She flipped the vegetables and meat over, checking their softness. Standing on her toes, she reached for a plate and a cup from the cabinet above the sink. She opened a drawer pulling out a knife and fork and took a single napkin from the napkin holder. She plated her meal, sprinkling salt and pepper on top of the flavourful food.

Annona walked towards the table with the hot dish in hand, her stomach grumbling with a vengeance. She placed the plate down in front of the chair, laying the utensils beside it. The seat she chose provided her with a view from her window. As she sat the grey skies turned into a purple haze, the blackened clouds drifting to pink.

Wanting to have a drink with her meal, she took ahold of her cup and returned to the jug of drinking water positioned beside the sink. She placed the cup under the spout, twisting the knob so that water would flow from it.

"The Ends of the Earth behind me, His Mark upon me, no turning back, no turning back."

Annona almost dropped her cup as her fingers fumbled with its grip. She swung her head to the radio as a grin stretched across her face. She couldn't recall the last time she heard the song, as it had been many seasons. She refused to fight back the tears that welled in her eyes. Through the watery vision she twisted the knob: the water from the faucet stopped. She blinked, sending hot tears down her cheeks.

"I have decided to follow the Artist, no turning back, no turning back."

Annona carried the cup of water to her seat while the song continued to play. She set the cup beside the food. Her free hand grasped the back of the chair as she leaned herself into a bowed position. The song continued to absorb her thoughts, taking her mind's eye to the day before she left Guardian's Ridge and moved to Desert's Stone. With her meal before her she paused, reflecting on the moment this song had became her battle cry.

When her time to leave for the Land of Rolling Hills was only a few weeks away, the reality of her Marking settled in, causing her heart to pound like a war drum, as if she was in the front lines heading into battle.

The questions her friends and family had been asking played like a broken record, the unknowns and fears repeating in her head. She was losing sight of the harvest. Her vision was clouded and she could only see the storms she was up against: starting over completely by herself.

Angō had laid its wired hands on her sweaty head and fixed its cables on her feet, clinging to her over the span of several days. It would let up merely for a few brief moments, indulging her to catch her breath, then reattaching itself once more. With Angō attached to her for weeks, the toughest burden was sleeping. Her vision blurred, she would imagine all the moments she would miss: family events, friendships, safety, and the comforts of her land. She imagined the worst things happening to her in the Land of Rolling Hills. But, for Annona it wasn't just her imagination playing tricks on her—she was convinced these fears would come true.

The unknown caused the greatest dread. She had no family or friends in the Land of Rolling Hills. No one had asked her to come, to help with a project, or provided her with the opportunity to harvest. Her first act of obedience to her Marking was to get there. The rest would have to follow suit.

Each night she would wrestle with Angō: the broken record of questions playing in her mind into the early hours of the morning, until her mind would give into exhaustion unable to think any longer, collapsing into a restless sleep.

She sensed little from the Artist during that time. She would call out to Him, sing to Him, and cry to Him, but there was no comfort given to her. This tightened the grip of Angō's wires on her head and made its cables like blocks of cement, weighing her down. She could only hear Angō's staticky voice telling stories of the worst scenarios imaginable, drowning out the Artist's voice, which was only a whisper away.

She sought solitude more than usual, finding solace in the forest amongst the wooden giants. Pine, oak, evergreen, and maple were some of the woods called wooden giants. Amongst the towering silence of the wooden giants Annona would find peace. The peace did not endure for long; more often than not it vanished by the time she had made it back to her home.

Reflecting on the day before her departure, Annona was beside herself with anguish. Angō's anxious words had chipped away any confidence she had once held. She contemplated that it still wasn't too late to remain in Guardian's Ridge. To never leave home. Had she really thought it all through? The idea bounced around in her troubled mind, offering itself as a solution to numb the worry. The anxiety. The loss of sleep. The agony. Surely this decision to leave Guardian's Ridge shouldn't cause such turmoil!

For the final time, Annona decided to head to the wooden giants—out of desperation. On this occasion she hiked deeper into the forest than she normally would.

She walked with Angō as it uttered an endless flow of mangled words, remarks that would lead her to fear and doubt, that permitted her no chance to interject amongst its lies.

"How do you *know* you can harvest? How are you so certain you need to go to the Land of Rolling Hills? Can you not harvest here?" Angō spat, relocating its cables and wires to make itself more comfortable. "The locals won't accept you. You won't find a place to harvest. You know you will leave everything just to realize that it was never supposed to be."

Angō no longer spoke, but rather screamed its words of anguish into her face. Its voice was all that she heard. She could no longer make out her own voice in her head, only her heart thumping: anxiety, fear. Anxiety, fear.

Angō hissed, "The Brothers visits were meaningless—they did nothing to produce character in you. The Artist sent them because you deserved the pain. He sent them to you because you have been a disappointment to Him." Angō was not told to stop, so it carried on, spewing its string of anxieties.

Annona's tired mind was spinning in a panic. She continued walking, one heavy foot in front of the other, making her way deep amongst the shadowing towers of the wooden giants. Knowing that she was nearing her landing place, Annona envisioned the refuge in her mind, her heart holding onto the image for hope. It was then that a light beamed, breaking through the wooden giants. Sticks snapped beneath her shoes. A wave of relief rippled through her flesh. That's when she saw it, like a lighthouse spotted amongst the stormy seas.

It wasn't much to look at. The first time she stumbled upon it she had almost missed it herself. She was certain if anyone cared to tread that far into the wooden giants, they would pass right by it. It was not like a mountain peak that promised a spectacular view nor the gentleness of a running stream that played a rhythm of restfulness. It was a simple field that broke amongst the woods, overlooking the tops of the wooden giants. The field had developed into a sacred place where she would find shelter to speak with the Artist. She called this place "The Altar." She had stumbled upon it some time ago while seeking refuge from the Brothers. For Annona, this was her courtroom where she had her uncensored conversations with the Artist. She would escape to The Altar when the waves of struggle, hardship, disappointments, failures, and even life refused to give Annona a moment to breathe. The Altar was a place that gave her breath, stopping her from drowning in the swell.

The Altar

The Altar was a break in the wooden giants where the hill dipped down, creating a large landing of a meadow. It appeared as if someone had taken a large blanket of luscious grass, and dropped it in the middle of the wooden giants. The grass grew thick and green—untouched. When the wind blew through the bare field, the long grass swooped down and flowed like waves of water, giving the appearance of the sea. Flowers speckled throughout the field, providing flecks of yellows and reds in-between the thick blades. The wooden giants surrounded the patch, like a fence. Annona liked to believe the wooden giants stood guard against the outer elements, providing her the protection and freedom to let her heart pour out to the Artist.

Whenever Annona arrived at The Altar, she made a point of removing her shoes; she knew she stood on holy ground.

Angō had permission to enter the field with her, but only because Annona had not demanded it to leave. Attached to her head and feet, it could penetrate any land.

Annona removed her shoes: first the right, then the left.

"I don't think the Artist will meet with you today. He has been silent," it said, squirming as Annona rose to her feet.

She arranged the shoes at the base of one of the wooden giants and made her way to the middle of the field. She sat down, folded her arms around her tucked knees, then thought better of it, adjusting to lie on her back, hands intertwined behind her head. The field, being situated on the side of a hill, granted her a view of the tops of the wooden giants, making her able to see for miles. She examined the blue sky, as two birds flew through her line of view, disappearing into the skyline.

Angō shifted itself repeatedly, ruthless in its tactics. "Getting more knowledge and learning more about the Land of Rolling Hills before moving there would be wiser. You've failed at learning a new tongue before; how will you be capable this time?" Angō insisted.

Angō's words of failure resounded like a clashing cymbal in her head.

"I need You, Artist," she whispered.

It started as a feeling, a tune stored in the back of her mind, playing itself quietly. She closed her eyes, urging the rustling sound out of the depths of her mind.

"Perhaps the Marking is wrong."

The tune slowly made its way to the forefront of her mind, the lyrics of the song sprinkling like water in her head.

"I have decided to follow Him, no turning back, no turning back."

Faint memories of Annona being tucked into bed, while her mother hummed the tune, vibrated to the forefront of her mind. She recalled singing the song in the Gallery, standing alongside her brothers and sisters. It was this very song she would commit herself to sing to the Artist when she was unwillingly carrying the Brothers, but also shouted it in the happiest of moments, when she would find her Relics and be overwhelmed with joy.

"The Ends of the Earth behind me, His Mark upon me, no turning back, no turning back."

The hum of the tune left her mind, the words resting on her tongue. She sang the words quietly, allowing each lyric of the song to slip past her lips.

"Though none go with me, still I will follow, no turning back, no turning back."

Angō shut its mouth, its wires losing its grip and slipping off of her head. Its cables loosened their clutch on Annona's feet. No longer able to only whisper the lyrics, she found her voice projecting the song from her diaphragm. It was a war cry—a declaration of her trust in the Artist—becoming her own anthem:

"I have decided to follow the Artist, no turning back, no turning back."

Annona sang the verses, repeating them until her voice was raw. Singing those lines over and over and over again, she sang until her physical body aligned with her newfound peaceful spirit. Overflowing her with renewed strength it gave her back her wings. Angō, who had completely discharged its wires and cables, shrivelled down to half its size and slithered away.

While Annona experienced the freedom that was poured upon her, she sang the words with conviction. Her mind cleared and visions of a great harvest flooded her thoughts, healing the parts of her mind that were distorted with Angō's smog of anxiety.

She knew in the Land of Rolling Hills, the Artist would take her feet to sights that were even greater than what was before her. She sang until the tears welled in her eyes, "Artist, I will go wherever You send me. I will love whoever You put in front of me. I will give to them whatever You need of me. Your servant is willing, send me."

Annona sat herself up, a smile shone across her face. She headed to the wooden giant that protected her shoes. She slipped them on, all the while humming her battle cry as she returned to her home. Renewed and restored, she was ready to head to the Land of Rolling Hills.

The crack of thunder rumbled through the hills of Annona's village. Snapping her eyes open, she focused on her food, returning to the present. The sound echoed through the village until it faded away; the tune ending on the final lyrics: *no turning back, no turning back*. She turned her focus to her dinner, her thoughts and memories of the wonderful peace she had experienced that day still played in her mind's eye.

"So be it," Annona said to herself. The declaration she declared at the Altar several seasons ago she again released to the Artist before she ate. Annona sat herself in the chair and enjoyed her meal. As she savoured the flavour of the vegetables, she stared at the changing skies displayed through her window. The skies beamed a fiery orange, as the clouds dissolved from light pink to a cherry red.

"So be it," she repeated to herself.

12

HER HEARTBEAT

Annona took the last bite of her meal, dabbing the meat on her fork against the oils that spread across her plate. She rose to her feet and took the dirty dishes to the sink, plunking them into the tub. She twisted the faucet on: the water gushing out as she squeezed a stream of soap into the sink.

Annona paused as the shallow tub filled, turning her back to the counter and leaning on the sink. She thought of what she desired to take care of this evening. She wanted to finish her letter to Hed, her dear friend who lived in Guardian's Ridge. More importantly, she expected a call from her family in the evening as she was waiting to receive an update of her Aunt's health.

Hed wrote to Annona often, asking questions about the Land of Rolling Hills, the harvest, and her Marking. Hed was not following her Marking, but she found it intriguing that Annona would pursue her own. The two of them enjoyed each other's company and the conversation of meaningful questions that would emerge when talking with one another.

As Annona washed the pots and dishes from dinner, she thought of the last letter that Hed had sent to her.

Hed's last letter asked Annona why she moved to the Land of Rolling Hills instead of trying to harvest in the Land of Four Seasons. Annona struggled with establishing her sentiments into words. Writing was a capability that did not flow naturally from her. When her friends or family urged her to write about her health or to provide news of the current events of the harvest, she would have to schedule times of seclusion. She would mull over her opinions and views, seeking to reveal the feelings tangled in her heart and mind.

Annona plunged the dish in the water, the bubbles engulfing the plate as it submerged into the bath. She drew the cloth from the holder and scrubbed on the sudsy plate. She proceeded to lather the soap onto the dishes, the suds foaming and frothing.

As the fizz splashed and lathered, Annona reflected, back to when she had first arrived in the Land of Rolling Hills and the excitement she experienced when she entered the land of her dreams.

Even though she had moved to the Land of Rolling Hills over four and a half rotations ago, she recalled the first few days of settling in as if it had taken place the day before. Her mind could summon both the significant and insignificant details within a moment's notice.

The Land of Four Seasons felt like another lifetime: a fading memory drifting into the abyss. So much had transpired since the time she left her home to her fourth season of harvest in the Land of Rolling Hills.

She faced many frustrations when she first arrived to the Land of Rolling Hills. Annona moved to a village called Desert's Stone, named for the relentless heat and the hard soil found in abundance. In appearance alone she was different from the crowd of locals. Remaining unnoticed was not something she could do, even amongst the mundane tasks, like going to the market or picking up supplies. The crowd would stop to stare at her, occasionally pointing at her with their mouths aghast. It developed into a constant reminder that no matter how hard she would try, by wearing the same style of clothing, shoes, or hair, she could not camouflage into the crowd. If she wanted to be accepted, she would have to show dedication, loyalty, and the willingness to sacrifice.

A separation between her and them would always exist, as the Land of Four Seasons and the Land of Rolling Hills had such a contrast in resources, infrastructure, and opportunities. Her privileged upbringing would prevent her from understanding what it was like to be raised in such harsh conditions. It was because of this adversity that the crowd of Desert's Stone showed such resilience towards the Brothers. They carried the Telaah and Peirasmos without resting; the Brothers rarely jumped off. The locals could glare at the Masters of Chaos and Suffering dead in the eye without releasing a shiver, capable of carrying them on their backs without showing strain. This innate resilience was only produced in one manor: to be born into a relentless environment where each day demanded survival.

When infrastructures had been neglected to be constructed for decades; when the soil was exposed, stripped, and extracted of its vegetation but not given new seeds; when the power-hungry continued to ransack the crowd of any resources or life-giving possessions; when the megalomaniac politicians merely saw with near sighted vision and not with the far-sighted vision needed for leaders of the land; when nations of the powerful and wealthy swooped in to exploit the workers of their gifting and talents only to replace it with machinery and imitations ... the next generation is forced to start over with what ever means remain. The next generation of the crowd is raised in a place plundered of its natural wealth, causing harsh conditions for survival and leaving little room for the luxury of creativity in work and passions. They must do whatever is demanded to ensure that they can feed their families, have shelter, and provide their children with education.

Creativity, options, opportunities, movement, choice, speech, freedom—all were privileges. Annona had always believed one had rights to these fundamental ideals, but coming to Desert's Stone changed that.

Watching how the crowd lived and recognizing that many in the crowd did not have these rights drastically shifted her perspective. She realized the crowd had no choice whether they wanted to live there or not. They were simply born into poverty. Her perspective deviated from the ignorance of not grasping that the majority of the Ends of the Earth lacked these basic needs.

The local crowd knew—and Annona knew—with a few swift messages to family and friends she could receive the finances needed to ensure food was on her table, or return to the Land of Four Seasons if there were ever a political uprising. The crowd of Desert's Stone, however, could not. It was this type of privilege that would always separate her from understanding what it was like to be born and raised without having the support and luxury of safety and resources.

Speaking in a new tongue was difficult for Annona. Her mind—so accustomed to speaking in her native tongue—stumbled, twisted, and blurted out incoherent words. Many times her attempt at saying something meaningful was met with confused stares. The kinder ones would nod in agreement despite the fact that she herself was confused by what she had just uttered.

The seasons also took getting used to. Annona was born in the Land of Four Seasons which, as the name states, had four seasons, while the Land of Rolling Hills had only two. In Annona's opinion, there was just one: hot. The scorching sun was relentless. Aside from the Scorching season, there was the Season of Tears, and with it would appear the clouds: large, boisterous, and full of water. In the morning chasing after the sun, they would form themselves so vast and magnificent, expanding like enormous bubbles. It looked as if an entire city could live inside just one of them. Hundreds of them would station themselves across the blue sky, and, like clockwork, wait for the evening to release the elements within.

Food was much more simple in Desert's Stone, providing plenty of nourishment, but lacking in creativity and flavour. It was not because the chefs from the Land of Rolling Hills weren't accomplished, as the land produced some of the most respected and sought after chefs. It was due to the deficit of harvest and cultivation of their vegetation. The land's first yields were shipped to nations of power, meeting the quota required in trade agreements. The excessive demand prevented them from being innovative, due to the scarcity of food.

Back in the Land of Four Seasons, family and friends lives carried on. Annona knew she was missing special moments and events in their lives; the distance between the Land of Rolling Hills and the Land of Four Seasons being far too great for her to travel back and forth as often as she would wish. Her close family was always kind to her. They understood and supported her desire to be in the Land of Rolling Hills, even coming to visit and volunteering to help with the harvest.

Despite all the struggling: the stumbling of the tongue, standing out amongst the crowd, the perpetual heat, lack of food, and missing family and friends, she'd do it ten thousand times over. It was absolutely, without doubt, worth it.

It was the innate, supernatural, indescribable, gut feeling she was in the right place.

Writing the letter to Hed

As Annona allowed herself to reflect on her magnetic pull to the Land of Rolling Hills, she was struck with the place to start in her letter to Hed, describing why she chose Desert's Stone. She set the final pot on the rack, releasing the murky water down the drain. Annona wiped her hands on the towel and flicked off the light. She made her way to her bedroom and sunk into her battered chair, resting her elbows on her desk. She slid open a drawer and took out a piece of paper, a pen, and Hed's letter. Annona cleared a surface on her desk to write on, skimmed over Hed's question, and began her response.

Dearest Hed,

You've asked me why I chose to harvest in the Land of Rolling Hills as opposed to harvesting in the Land of Four Seasons. I can do my best to explain why, but I am convinced the best approach to answer why is to shed light on the 'what'. 'What' it is that draws me in; 'what' it is that makes me feel alive; 'what' it is the Land of Rolling Hills offers in contrast to what the Land of Four Seasons does not.

So, what draws me in? It is the land, deep and mountainous, with peaks reaching far into the purple and blue skies. Dehydrated mud that begs to be worked, turned, shovelled, and picked... so dry it is like cement to the touch, but beneath the hard exterior it is enriched with mineral soil that is begging to be surfaced. Wooden giants stretching high to the sky, the leaves like hands pleading to the heavens, determined they will open and release the promised waters from the swollen clouds. Rivers that resemble the flowing veins on the back of an Elder's thinned hand; the crowd who wash their worn clothing and gather water for the day, while the pigs and cows governed by the farmer's rod are only a few feet further upstream, bathing themselves, struggling to uncover a sanctuary from the sun. Stars—the brilliant, awe-inspiring, uncountable stars—stretching themselves across the dark blanket of the night sky, and the moon that illuminates the path like a lamp for the hard workers who are just returning home from the fields.

The huts, with their dirt floors, and the black, stained, rusted pots. The water that has been resting inside the blue gallon buckets used for bathing and cleaning: the liquid turned green due to the harsh sun and the stale movement. The worn blankets spread out across the floor that both serve as mattresses and as warmth in the cool evenings. The pictures of missed loved ones: faded, mounted in simple black frames, and hung on the wall between images of beautiful heavens from a distant homeland—the scene overlaid with cursive verses of peace and prosperity inscribed on them.

The smells that greet you as you make your way to the village's heart; the potent smell of burning rubber and trash that stings your eyes, but is whisked quickly aside and the senses soothed by the aroma of foreign spices and cooked meats that are being peddled on the streets.

It is the mother's hands: wiry, calloused, leathered, scarred, and cracked from the thousands of hours of labour, yet still a hand that is soft and familiar to her children as it brings soothing comfort to the distressed mind. The dirty, faded, and torn apron she wears each day—to the rich only rags—but to all mothers like her the apron a gown of roles... the most precious article of a uniform that speaks of her thankless work. The apron states she is her family's anchor: their doctor when one is sick; a chef who will beat the sunlight each morning to prepare a delicious breakfast for her children, and who will sacrifice her own portion so that her household can eat until their stomachs have had their fill; a merchant who will leave to sell goods in the markets; the maid who will clean their home and will not sleep until long after the moon has shown her face; and a poet who finds time every day to express her thankfulness of provision to the Artist. She insists her own children must pursue their Marking, sacrificing anything she can to secure that they might experience a life without the Brother's weighing on their shoulders.

The children's eyes, their curiosity peaked by our outward distinctions. Dancing with reckless spontaneity. Laughter and giggles loaded on the tips of their tongues, and the songs that are sung like a chorus. The wiggling, waving, clapping, and jumping: they perform whenever they are given an opportunity to shine. Eagerness to impress, to recite what they have learned, and to reveal to you what their secret talent is.

This is the tip of a mountain-sized iceberg, a single scene out of a film, or a verse from a psalm of what draws me in. The Land of Four Seasons has forgotten the beauty of simplicity; it is no longer delighted with the acts of kindness, hospitality, or gratefulness, but shrugs with apathy and entitlement when gifted with acts of self-lessness.

She is like a whale who's mouth is invariably open, swallowing whatever appears in her path to satisfy the gnawing hunger in her stomach. But, we both recognize it will never satisfy her. Her mouth agape, ever yearning for more: the newest, the greatest, the smartest, the strongest, and the richest. It is a way of existence I find exhausting, when it consumes me (and it does, in a mere matter of time). It spins me round and round until I am so distracted that I no longer can distinguish myself from the selfish whale. Everything that I vow I will not want, I become; I am the starving whale who demands more and more!

If I could denounce my allegiance to my homeland I would. I am ashamed that for much of my life I took part in the stuffing down and muting of the impoverished voices. I am guilty. Guilty for having a part in projects and purchasing materials that are sourced from the spilling out of their blood.

The Land of Rolling Hills invites you into a life of simplicity. Titles and papers we slap upon ourselves, that offer us self-worth and identity, they do not bear the same magnitude here. What is admired and sought after is the character of the individual, their willingness to abandon their own desires to help the crowd. The

Land of Rolling Hills is not absorbed with a life of business, routines, and projects. It welcomes you to leave behind the multiple chores we place on ourselves to appear productive and to keep up with others. Instead it allows you to focus—being present—on one meaningful project at a time. With the limitation in resources, it awakens your mind to finding innovative solutions based on what you have within your grasp, not relying on a machine to overcome the obstacle for you.

The crowds of the Land of Rolling Hills come together as one when inflicted by the Brothers: when one mourns, all bear the burden of tears and suffering. When one is hungry, all seek to find bread for him, gathering together whatever resources they might have to satisfy his empty stomach. When one thirsts, they all take to the river to gather water to quench his dryness.

I have witnessed the most daring acts of bravery in standing testament to the stories of resilience, resourcefulness, and kindness from the local crowd. Harrowing stories of ruthless conditions and perseverance beyond comprehension! Within them, a deep reservoir of strength is found. When confronted with poverty, lack of food, or unsuitable shelter, they nevertheless give whatever they have to one another so that no one might suffer alone.

Each day I find myself amongst some of the most humble, resilient, caring, and generous beings. In my opinion, sadly, some of the most silenced, abused, neglected, and oppressed. Yet I know, one day the Artist will place them in the seat of honour, and those who have given themselves the authority to rule over and dominate now, have already received their compensation in full.

Evidently they have something we lack: gratefulness. Gratefulness: the skilled ability to be thankful for whatever is in their possession—trusting that the Artist has already provided for their need, it has already been released, and that the Artist will reveal it to them in due time.

This is my 'why', Hed. My heartbeat. It's why I choose the Land of Rolling Hills, so that maybe one day, should I learn to strip myself of my selfish desires, I might produce even in the slightest, the hard-learned dexterity of resilience, generosity, gratefulness, and kindness; to possess something that mirrors these traits!

Annona tossed the pen down, rubbing her temples as her eyes drifted out of focus. She reread her letter, tweaking the grammar and spelling, until her response to Hed satisfied her. She folded the letter, placed it in the envelope addressed to her friend, and stuffed it inside her satchel to drop off at the post after work.

Annona checked the time, still expecting a call from her mother that evening. She expected her to call earlier but understood the situation back in the Land of Four Season was painful for her family. Her mother had revealed to her a few days prior that her Aunt was sick. As soon as her mother informed her of this, she noticed the weight of the Brothers climbing on her back and clasping to her legs. She tried to shake them off, but once again they were too heavy.

13

HARVESTING

As she waited at her desk for her family to call, she found her hands occupied by the first harvesting tool she used when she had arrived in Desert's Stone. Jore had given her the tool to gauge the nutrients in the soil. Jore and Annona became good friends ever since he invited her to harvest in Desert's Stone, taking her under his wing to teach her the customs of the culture and easing her into the work of the fields. Many of the tools he had packed away and retired found a second life when he gave them for her to use. Annona used the hand-gauger daily, as it helped the Planters and Harvesters to decide which fields carried specific minerals, reporting which vegetation would yield the greatest volume in the specific soil.

Annona rotated the measuring apparatus, noting the faded script and the splintered handle. She had cracked the screen of the gauge that measures the minerals, accidentally dropping it on the path from the fields to her home during her third rotation around the sun. When she saw the shattered screen, she knew she'd have to acquire another device. Too attached to the gauger to throw it out, it reminded her of when she had first arrived to Desert's Stone, and it had became a memento of her new beginning.

Annona's fear of not locating a place to harvest dissipated on the first day of her move to Desert's Stone. The evening when Annona had moved into her home, rumours were circulating throughout the village that one Marked Harvester had arrived. The next day she awoke to a loud knock on her door. She tiptoed across the tiled floor, bumping into furniture and boxes she had not yet unpacked. Squinting through her front window, and in the dawn's early light, she saw one of the crowd knocking on her front door.

She went to the door, slowly opening it to a small crack. Immediately she was drawn to his Marking, Planter. His eyes were the shapes of crescent moons; the colour as dark as the eclipse. He had a smile across his face, the kind of smile that made you wonder what he knew that you didn't. His skin was dark, weathered from the sun, and his attire was faded and worn from the mud. He spoke to Annona in Desert Stone's native tongue. Annona's eyes widened and returned his cyphered code with a blank stare. Without missing a beat he switched to Annona's tongue of origin, speaking without an accent.

"I'm sorry, I wasn't sure if you spoke Desert's Stone's dialect."

Annona felt heat rise in her cheeks. "Oh, yeah, unfortunately I do not."

Jore asked Annona questions about her travels, asking her why she chose Desert's Stone. Within a few minutes they were speaking as friends—a natural ease flowed between them.

"So you're a Harvester?"

Annona nodded her head. "Well, yes." She hesitated, wanting to explain that she would need guidance to start. "I've received my Marking but have no experience in harvesting. I just knew I had to come here, to the Land of Rolling Hills, and the rest would follow."

Jore smiled, pushing his hands into his pockets. "We all have to start somewhere," he said, nodding his head toward a dirt road beyond

Annona's front yard. "Just a few kilometres down the road, not far—you can't miss it—is a farm. There's a group of us, Harvesters and Planters. We've been there for several seasons, and we're well established in planting and cultivating." A muscle tightened in his jaw. "However, we don't have enough Harvesters. We're desperate. Word around the village is that one Marked Harvester had arrived, so an Elder sent me to seek you out. We'd love for you to join us."

As the words left Jore's mouth and reached Annona's ears, she felt a raw excitement stirring in her chest. She did not believe in coincidences, but purely in divine appointment. She replied yes before asking questions about the production, her instincts telling her that destiny just knocked on her door.

Her abrupt yes proved not to be Annona's wisest move. When she reported to the field the next morning, she realized that Jore's choice of word "desperate" was a gross understatement. An entire season passed of Annona sorting through the vines and weeds that had ravaged and choked the vegetation. In the midst of sorting, she uncovered crop that was severely under-picked. Most of the vegetation had grown rampant and was intertwined with weeds. The crops had to be meticulously catalogued by given proper labelling. Some of the production was harvested, while other fields of vegetation were stripped and burned. Setting the fields on fire would have provided the fields a fresh start and was also a common practice in Desert's Stone. But, some of the vegetation was still edible, and the Elders believed it was a waste to burn the harvest, no matter how small. When the arduous work of sorting and extracting finished, the fields were ready to be sown with new seeds. Annona worked alongside the Planters to design a sequence adopted for sowing, allowing the harvest to be more bountiful and restoring the fields to order.

A sudden chirp from the gauger snapped Annona from reminiscing and returned her to the present. Annona clicked a button. It beeped back at her, informing her there was life within the old wires. The screen had a back-light that would make the face easier to interpret when handling outdoors, especially when operated under the bright sun. Darkness rolled into Annona's room; the dial illuminated like a flashlight. Annona tried to read the screen, but the large cracks made it illegible. A pressure spot had blackened part of the screen. Annona sighed, placing the gauger back on her desk. She glanced at the phone, willing it to ring, but no one was waiting for her on the other end. Out of boredom she returned her gaze to the measuring instrument. Stacked beside the gauger were several textbooks. Some contained information about seeds and soil, others about extracting and replacement. The Elders gave these books to all the Planters and Harvesters. Reading the texts was mandatory. The material developed and strengthened the abilities the Marked possessed and taught them to recognize the gifting within their team.

Annona picked the text titled "The Simple Seed." Akim, one of the Elder Harvesters, passed it on to her in her third season of harvest.

When she had first met Akim, his demeanour immediately took her aback. Never before had she met someone so calm, kind, and grounded. He was steadfast in the Artist's love, and this confidence emanated from every aspect of him. Jore explained to her upon first introductions that Akim had harvested in the Land of Rolling Hills for over twenty rotations around the sun. Although the sunspots and weathered skin gave away his time spent in the fields, the way he spoke of the locals and his approach to work did not. He approached his work with child-like eagerness. He spoke only kindness about the residents of Desert's Stone, never showing a hardened heart nor hostility.

In contrast to his kindness, his face was harsh: he had a snow-white beard he kept neatly trimmed close to his face, except for his chin and lower jaw, allowing the beard to have volume and form into a perfect "v" shape. A patch of black hair streaked jaggedly down from the centre of his lower lip to his chin, resembling a trail on the side of a mountain. He had a crooked nose, eyes sunken deep into his head. The colours of his glossy eyes were like marbles with a chestnut centre. His hair—the same colour of his beard—was brushed back from his forehead. He stood tall and slender; his bony cheeks peaked through his tightened skin when he would clench his jaw, which was a perpetual habit of his. This tick piqued when problem solving or trying to work out a dilemma. His jaw bone clenched and relaxed, perturbing and disappearing. He wore a similar outfit each day: a blue shirt with black jeans, boots laced to his calves. He walked with a limp, to an onlooker it appeared as if he was shuffling. Jore explained to Annona that it was due to an injury when he first arrived to the fields.

On her first interaction with him she felt nervous, afraid he would be the type who would desire ruthless devotion and loyalty firstly to him, and secondary to the work in the fields. But, the opposite proved true: he cared more about the Marked in front of him, wanting to know them and their talents. He was a quiet leader; he served humbly. In return, the Marked serving in the fields gave their loyalty to him without him ever having to ask for it.

He asked Annona of her Relics, her Masterpiece, what her interaction with the Painter was like. She told him how he had transitioned into a storm, and Akim chuckled at this, stating that the Painter had done something similar to him too.

His voice was deep like the reverberating sound of a voice spoken into a well. Yet, it was hoarse, even raspy, like he was constantly recovering from a cold. The combination of sounds worked well together. When Akim spoke it captivated the attention of the crowd before him.

Although Annona's interactions with Akim were not daily, they were enough for her to come to deeply respect him, both as a leader and as a friend.

So when Akim passed the text book to Annona, suggesting she skim through it, Annona read each word on each page, from cover to cover.

The book defined the expertise of the Planters. The text gave Annona a greater respect for their skill sets and abilities, significantly increasing her confidence in their decision making.

She leafed through the pages, her eyes skipping over the highlighted text:

The Planters are knowledgeable of the seed. They understand the seed is composed of three parts: the embryo, endosperm, and the testa. They identify which seeds will provide shrubbery, wooden giants, flowers, and which will produce fruit or vegetation.

Effortlessly, they can penetrate the appropriate grade of depth for the seed, and additionally, have the expertise to provide the seed the exact distance required between their fellow plants.

Planters can recall types of shrubbery, fruit, and vegetation by examining the seed, and an experienced Planter can analyze the species of plant from a stem just sprouted from the earth.

The Harvesters are gifted in nurturing vegetation. They find it easy to extract the yield as they have an eye for deciphering when the crop has reached its peak.

Harvesters and Planters must work closely as one, for one working without the other will not produce the same yield. One without the other will not bring the harvest to its full glory. Without the two working harmoniously, the true harvest will be suppressed in the soil, unable to bring itself to its foretold potential.

Annona closed the book and tossed it to the centre of her desk. The chair squealed in protest as she reclined, stretching her legs out in front of her, lacing her hands behind her head as she mulled over the text.

Annona reflected on her own team. They worked alongside the Planters, trading information to help each other in the areas the others lacked in.

The atmosphere among the Harvesters and the Planters was one of encouragement and care for one another. Gratitude was shown for the knowledge that the others excelled in, void of behaviours of jealousy.

Neither group of the Marked felt like one Marking was more significant than the other. The team of workers knew they needed to work harmoniously in order for the harvest to be plentiful. When they worked in unison, they produced more. If they produced more, Desert's Stone would be the receiver of the 'chain reaction of good'. The more vegetation produced by the Planters and Harvesters, the more product was available to the vendors. The vendors sold the plentiful vegetation at a lower cost as there were greater quantities. Product would be traded with surrounding villages for the natural resources they produced. This provided a better income for the families, and more food on their tables. Families were able to focus on life beyond mere survival.

A seed grown in darkness

It wasn't just food they grew in Desert's Stone—they cultivated hope. A simple seed of hope, buried into the darkness of sorrow.

Seasons passed, storms came, the sun shone, and their faith would refuse to tremble. To others, it was bleak. Unable to see, they refused to believe. But, those familiar with the Brothers, who had their feet settled in the Artist, understood what this meant. Waiting was a requirement; to endure, to persevere through the storm. To determine to stand firm when there was no evidence their circumstance would change. The sufferers steadied themselves for the seed of hope, believing it would do what it was meant to do: grow. And, it would. It always did. It would burst forth from the soils of sorrow, the sprouts of leaves and a stem. The plant was the tangible truth that hope prevails—is resurrected—through darkness. Although it could be buried, snuffed out, even thrown into the depths of the earth, darkness would not have the final word. Hope would always overcome.

Annona looked at the telephone, willing it to ring. But, her family wasn't on the other end. She pulled herself forward, the chair again squealing as her arms reached in front of her for the textbook. She took the book into her hands and settled it at the base of the tower of literature.

Tick, tick, tick, tick.

Annona marvelled at her watch, listening to the faint clicking of the minute hand rotating around the clock's face.

Before moving to the Land of Rolling Hills she had never owned a watch. To her, time was pliable and transient: a mere suggestion of hours and minutes that was not powerful enough to dictate her daily routines. However, after being gifted this watch during her second season in the fields from Akim and Chayim, she rarely took it off.

Annona recalled the moment fondly; it was a beautiful sunny day, the wind stronger than usual. Hidden behind layers of clouds was the sun, every so often peaking through the masses. Annona had completed a third of her daily duties. Focussing on reaping, she moved methodically through the wheat fields, selecting the grains that were arching that showed no signs of green. The wheat would be collected and stored, then bagged and sent to the neighbouring villages.

"Annona."

Annona turned to see Akim approaching her. His hair was covered with a light layer of dust. The sun, beaming behind him, gave an illusion of a reddish tint to his hair. As he approached Annona, he wore a smile across his tanned face. Beside him was another Elder, a Planter named

Chayim, who had unlatched her seed satchel from her waist, now carrying it by her side.

Annona returned the smile to both. Leaving the wheat attached to the soil, she walked toward them.

"A beautiful day, isn't it?" Chayim said to Annona.

Annona looked to the skies, noting the hundreds of cumulus clouds. "It is," Annona replied.

Akim looked at the row that Annona had been extracting. "This has been a bountiful season—one to remember." Akim broke off a head of wheat and placed it in his mouth. The kernels made a loud crunching sound, another sign that the harvest was indeed ready for reaping.

Annona nodded her head in agreement. Having only completed two seasons of harvesting, she was unsure what a scarce production looked like. Akim shifted his weight, looking at Chayim. He gave a small nod. Chayim reached into her pocket, producing a small, shiny item. She offered it to Annona. As Annona extended her hand to receive the trinket, Akim began to speak.

"We wanted to get you something: a small gift as a token of our appreciation."

Annona's brow furrowed as she looked into the palm of her hand. It was a watch: a gold rimmed face with a leather band. The face was white and the numbers: roman numerals—a detail Annona immediately appreciated.

"This is for me?" Annona asked.

"Yes, something from all of the Elders. It's not much—just a small way we can show our gratitude."

Annona felt deeply moved by the gesture. Her eyes began filling with tears. Her lower lip quivered as she fought to find the words to show her gratitude. "Thank you," was all Annona could manage to say between the tears.

"You're more than welcome," Chayim replied, smiling as she glanced over at Akim.

Annona opened her arms to Chayim, hugging and thanking her. As she released her, Chayim centred her hand on Annona's Marking and stepped back. Annona embraced Akim. For the brief moment he held her there, Annona felt secure. He smiled as she pulled away from him, his hand centred on her Marking. Annona squinted to make out Akim's Marking; it was so worn and embedded into his skin that upon first glance, one would think he had not been Marked. His Marking had become faded, no longer an identifier.

"We'll let you get back to it," Akim said, placing his hand on her shoulder. He and Chayim turned and walked away. As Annona watched them leave, she admired the band once more, taking in each detail. She wrapped the stiff band around her wrist, sliding the leather through the gold latch.

Now, as Annona sat in her desk, she noticed the leather and how it had darkened from sweat and dirt. The leather had become soft. The glass of the watch face still remained unscratched, with hints of oxidization around the gold rim that showed its exposure to the elements. But, she preferred the watch in its current form: showing signs that it was well-worn. In the first few days of wearing the watch, she had keenly felt its presence against her skin. The materials felt foreign to her. But, now, she no longer noticed it, for it had become part of her. It was when she would forget her watch at home, suddenly realizing the missing weight from her wrist, that she felt bare.

Annona looked out the window: the skies dark and the stars shining overhead. A wave of exhaustion washed over Annona. A sudden yawn rose within her, escaping from her lips as she tried to push the drowsiness away.

Each day, the Harvesters and the Planters would do what their hands, their heart, and their mind gave itself naturally to. Each day, when they would open their eyes from their wake, the drowsiness would quickly melt away because there was good work needing to be done. And at night, when they laid their heads to sleep, rest would come easily because good work had been done.

Wheat ready for harvest

The phone rang, snapping Annona out of her lethargy. Reality waited on the other end to shake her to her core.

14

AUNT'S MASTERPIECE

Sickness is merciless and has no care for its subjects. It infests itself how it wants: chaotically, randomly. Illness has no regard for time, no preference for the rich nor poor, does not discriminate against the tone of skin, nor the land of origin. Like the Brothers, sickness surrounds itself to whoever it wants.

Annona worried for her Aunt as she anticipated the news. Her mother told her about the digression of her Aunt's health, modern medicine could not bring the holistic healing she needed.

Sickness and diagnosis, funerals and births, weddings and parties... it was these life-events that would remind her how far away she was from Guardian's Ridge. Annona found ways to cheat the distance, using modern technology to communicate with her family to help close the gap. But, these events blew the gap wide-open, revealing a terrifying chasm of distance between her and her family.

She had devoted the rest of the night to going over her Aunt's health with her family and taking a check on her family's heart beat. They reassured Annona that for the night, her Aunt was stable and her health would hold steady over the next few days. Her family insisted they would call should anything change. With the storm calmed, Annona prepared herself for bed. She settled her head to rest and talked with the Artist until she fell asleep. It was as if she were in a boat: the waves rocking her to a state of calmness, then rest.

Just as the weather takes no commands from the crowd, the storm brewed throughout the night. The next morning, a call awoke Annona, the waters that were once rhythmic grew chaotic once again, the sound of thunder resounded in the distance. Before picking up the phone, she guessed what news was on the other end. Hesitantly, she answered, bracing herself for the impact.

The storm unleashed her fury, the waves crashing into her. Her boat was sinking. Her Aunt, a giant in pursuing her Marking, who had dedicated her life to the most beautiful Masterpiece, had passed. She passed quietly in the night during her sleep. Annona knew she was already with the Artist—in the arms of the Sculptor.

Her Aunt, who was tenderly loved, was more than an inspiration for Annona. She challenged Annona to love without boundaries or restrictions. She did not achieve this by lecturing the crowd, nor by establishing herself on a platform to preach at anyone who crossed her path. The love she wished others to experience came out of her so contagiously and radiantly. Her reputation spoke for her: she quietly and confidently lived a life of selfless love.

Her Aunt's life story began with so much anguish and hostility. She was born into a family that did not accept her, forcing her to make herself invisible to avoid conflict. Her family looked upon her as "less than" compared to her siblings. Family is designed to be the safest place you can turn to, where you are always met with unconditional love and acceptance. But, she was not provided this from them. Defiantly, they withheld the foundational right of family—the right to love and to be loved.

One of the cruelest acts that can be done is not what one inflicts intentionally, but it is what one refuses to give: withholding love, withholding acceptance, and withholding respect.

Her Aunt would have had every reason to be miserable, or hostile—even angry. Any judge would have granted her permission to cut them out of her life, or at least keep them at an arms length.

Yet, triumphantly, as a pioneer blazing her own trail, she traveled the path that is seldom pursued. Her Aunt would not allow hatred to have say in her life, not even a whisper. She chose each day to love and forgive. She determined, in every moment, to see her transgressors not as bullies or opposer, but as a result of brokenness manifested from the Ends of the Earth, due to the lack of those following their Marking.

She loved the broken, encouraged others to love, and she modeled forgiveness. Annona couldn't recall a time when she saw her Aunt sad or angry, only showing her sadness when telling of the ones who were absorbed by their own brokenness. She was one who spent hours conversing with the Artist and who genuinely knew Him. Who better to teach her a life of love than the Potter: familiar with suffering, close to the afflicted, and rejected among the crowd. She knew He understood. This is where her Aunt received her endless supply of strength and wisdom.

Annona would love to talk with her Aunt about what her hands, her heart, and her mind would give itself naturally to, because her Aunt would bless her, speak words of life over her, and encourage her to pursue her Marking. Her Aunt understood Annona's desire to go to the Land of Rolling Hills, as she herself traveled to the Land of Heat in pursuit of her own Marking.

Now with her gone from the Ends of the Earth, her Aunt was dancing in the rivers of joy and basking in the sun of perfect peace where Love Conquers All.

Annona recalled the last time she had seen her Aunt's Masterpiece. Splattered in the left corner were colours that conflicted: greys, dark yellows, and greens. The colours combined were visually unpleasing, the strokes of paint were jagged and sharp. Annona asked her Aunt why she didn't request the Painter to cover the colours. Annona was certain He would do that for her.

Her Aunt smiled at her and said, "A beautiful painting that shows no ugliness bears no contrast. One looks at them, and presumes they were always graceful. They see them at face value. However, beauty displayed by the ugliness forced into my life shows better than the solitary beauty of ten thousand hand-picked roses. You see the origin in which it came from, along with what it has grown to become. That's what the Artist did for me: He took the darkness that was forced upon me and produced something extraordinarily beautiful out of it."

Even with this dear memory that would remain eternally in her mind and heart, Annona still sensed the weight of the Brothers bearing down on her. Angō came and plunged its wires in to her head with its cables latched on her feet. Thoughts of her family mourning in her absence was troubling. She wrestled with her spirit, wondering if it was time to return to Guardian's Ridge.

What she couldn't wrap her mind around was her lack of tears; she didn't understand why she was not crying. Dread and worry stormed over her, but she couldn't release the emotions from within.

Restlessly, Annona muttered a prayer to the Artist, urging Him to give peace, reassurance, and hope to her family.

Unsure of what to do next, she performed mechanically. She donned her boots, snatched up her jacket, and headed to the fields. On the road, Akim crossed her path. As Annona told Akim what had happened, his eyes filled with tears and he placed his arm firmly around her shoulder. In silence, he walked with her, weighing on Annona as he limped beside her. His strong and steadfast presence gave peace to Annona as they reached the fields.

Annona needed to first stop at the workshop to assemble her tools. Before they parted, Akim took Annona's arm, guiding her to face him. He lifted his hand and blessed her with grace and peace, then placed his hand over her Marking.

Placing one's hand over the Marking was an unfamiliar practice for

Annona. Elders explained it acknowledged the physical amongst the spiritual. The seen amongst the invisible. The reality amongst the mystical—that even though it was unseen, the Artist was in the midst of it all. The act recognized the decision and sacrifice they made to follow their Marking.

Akim placed his calloused and cracked hand upon Annona's Marking. The pure act quieted her anxiousness and stilled her worries. Akim nodded, slowly withdrew his hand, and walked away.

Annona pushed past the door, entering the workshop to grab her shovel. She resolved to begin the day by inspecting the harvest. The word of her Aunt's passing reached the workers that Akim passed in the fields. With such a small community of workers, sharing in each other's pains and joy was a common understanding.

Annona took the shovel and walked to the counter to find a measuring device. She took the device into her hand and proceeded to the back door. Pulling on the handle, she stepped outside and headed towards the narrow pathways that led to the acres of fields. Annona saw Jore cutting through the field, making his way to her. Akim must have told him, too.

"Annona, what are you doing here?" Jore came up to her and wrapped his arms around her.

Annona wasn't sure how to explain. "I don't know what else to do. It just... it doesn't seem real." Annona regretted her decision of coming to work, realizing she should have remained at home. She didn't want to face the others and explain why she had come to work, and to listen to dozens of Planters and Harvesters offer their condolences when she hadn't even released her own tears.

Jore released her from his arms, his face turned solemn. "I lost my cousin a few seasons back. He passed suddenly. He wasn't even sick." Jore's face stiffened. He smiled so often, it seemed out of place to see him so serious.

"I remember getting the news from my mother. I sat on the other end of the phone, silent. It didn't feel real. She asked me if I was okay, I told her I was. I spoke with his parents and siblings. I missed the funeral because it was difficult to get back to my village. At that time, I thought I was doing the right thing." Jore discovered a rock on the ground, he rolled it under his boot, avoiding Annona's eyes.

"I loved him so dearly. He taught me so many lessons in life. Quick to forgive, slow to anger, laughed at himself, and loved everyone who came across his path so deeply." Jore stopped kicking the rock and looked at Annona, his eyes brimmed with tears.

"I didn't experience his loss until much later, when I returned to my village. When I had learned my cousin had passed, my mind could not fathom that he was gone. I carried on my life like nothing had changed and acted like everything was normal. When I traveled back to my village for a sabbatical, I went to visit my cousins and his parents in their home," Jore said, sniffling, his eyes back on the rock. "I kept waiting for my cousin to walk into the room, to greet me with one of his massive bear hugs. It wasn't until that moment that I experienced the absence of his presence and fully comprehend that he was gone. That's when my grief struck me. My family had entered the process of healing while I hadn't yet begun to mourn."

Jore shook his head and placed his hands inside his pockets. "Grief comes in many states, but seldom is it spoken of how it holds back: retreating momentarily until it will inevitably be unleashed."

Annona swallowed the lump growing inside her throat. She nodded her head in silent agreement.

"Take all the time you desire, Annona. Do whatever works for you. Go back to the Land of Four Seasons, or rest in your house. If you can't do these things and you think harvesting will keep your mind occupied, you are welcome to do that too. Or even tag along with me today, I can show you some plantings we've been working on." Jore raised his eyes to Annona, and gave a half smile while giving Annona another hug, longer this time, as if to say "I feel it too."

He let her go, squeezing her hands as he headed towards the fields. Annona paused for a moment and weighed her options. She knew Angō blurred her vision, so she demanded it to release her. It immediately retreated at her spoken command.

With her mind clear, she sucked back air, held her breath while counting backwards from five, then gently released it out of her nose. Her eyes watching Jore's silhouette, she followed behind him, with her shovel rotating in her hands.

15

BREAKING BREAD

Annona checked the health of the harvest, making a path through each row, reviewing the condition of the yield. The Elders gave the task of overseeing the fields to Annona. Through its preventative means, the inspections acted as a safety precaution so that any harmful weeds could be immediately extracted. The task was given to her in her third season of harvest.

Several weeks passed since her Aunt had passed away. The steadiness of work provided Annona with enough distraction to prevent her from accepting the magnitude of such a great loss. On several occasions, she appeared overwhelmed by her work, resulting in more periods of rest. But, as each day passed, she felt herself transition back into her daily routine.

With such an immense volume of crop that season, it had been several weeks since Annona had the chance to get back into the wheat and barley fields to inspect for any abnormal growths.

As Annona lifted the leaves to examine the stems earthed in the dirt, she caught a weed leeched to the base of the plant. She plucked it from the plant, tossing it into the basket she wore as a backpack, afterward to be disposed of and burned.

"That's odd," Annona spoke to herself as she went through the surrounding wheat. At the base of each stalk was an identical weed.

"Annona!" She heard Jore's voice bouncing from behind her. Crouched over, she turned to see Jore walking between the rows towards her.

"Hey, Jore!" She yelled back, returning her focus to the vegetation, removing another weed and throwing it into her basket. She heard the crunch of his boots as he approached her.

"What do you got there?"

"Wish I could tell you, but I have no clue."

Jore bent down beside Annona, surveying the weed she extracted from the wheat stalk.

"That's odd, I've never seen a weed like this, either."

"That's not good," Annona said, passing the weed over to Jore for a second opinion. "They're attached to the base of the stems of the vegetation, twisting around the roots. It looks like it has affected this entire row."

Jore flipped the weed over, viewing the root and the three pointed leaves that sprouted from it.

"I'll run tests the morning after Selah to see if it can be identified. I'm certain it's nothing, just a common weed," Jore said, tucking the weed inside the pouch of his backpack. "It's close to dusk, we're supposed to go to Akim's tonight to break bread." Jore rose to his feet, extending his hand to Annona as he helped her up.

"Oh, right. I had forgotten about that." Annona smiled, knowing that was not true. On the eve of every Selah, the Elders took turns hosting a meal together. They used these hours to welcome the day of rest and reflection, giving a pause to the never-ending work.

Jore looked unimpressed, yet playful. "Yeah, right!" he laughed, lifting his eyebrow to her. Annona grinned as she wiped her hands, the loose dirt falling to the ground. Annona loved breaking bread with the Elders and the Marked. The meal not only provided rest from the heaviness of their work, but also gave opportunity to bond within their community of Planters, Harvesters, and Elders.

Akim knew that a heaviness would fall on the Marked after they made it past their first few seasons of harvest. Being surrounded by poverty becomes draining, when one problem is solved several more are discovered. On the way to and from the fields, the workers would be stopped by the crowd of Desert's Stone and asked to provide money, food, or shelter. Feelings of despair, believing the job was too significant, or ceasing to believe change was possible were all common causes for the Planters and Harvesters to abandon their Marking. To counteract this, Akim started communal dinners each week to celebrate all the victories that were taking place. Elders shared their wisdom. The Planters and Harvesters talked about their families at home. Singing, dancing, praising the Artist, and talking about their families were the highlights of these nights. As the local Gallery was designated for the crowd of Desert's Stone, this act of community and breaking of bread was their team's equivalent to attending the Gallery.

Jore and Annona walked together to Akim's house, collecting workers scattered in the fields along the way.

Akim's house was located just outside of Desert's Stone. He had constructed the house of brick, the style complementary with the other homes surrounding it.

As they approached the house, the door was open: welcoming all to gather inside. Jore, Annona, and the others made their way into the interior of the home as Akim received them in the kitchen.

"Good evening, and shalom," Akim said, carrying a cutting board with a loaf of bread in one hand and a bottle of wine in the other.

"Shalom," Annona said in unison with the others.

"We will sit outside in the courtyard tonight. If some could help to bring the platters on the counters, I would be most grateful," Akim said. Spread on the counter were arrangements of food. Annona, along with the others, helped to bring the items to the back end of the house, following Akim as he strolled with a small limp.

Akim had prepared a spread of food and drinks. Most of the Elders and the workers were already present, deep in conversation. Laughter erupted from the late arrivers as the Elders and Marked who had arrived on time teased them about the influence of polychronic time.

Playful banter carried on as Annona approached where the well stood, beyond the courtyard. The refreshing liquid splashed against her dry skin as she washed her hands and face.

As Annona washed her hands, she admired the beautiful layout that Akim had arranged. The spread was simple, void of vintage flatware or silver cutlery. The food was neither imported nor luxurious, but the charm was in the community of the Marked: the laughter that rose like a sweet perfume, the smiles that sparkled like diamonds, and the words of kindness and encouragement that reverberated like a composer's symphony. *Priceless.*

Jore motioned for Annona to sit beside him. She grinned as he shuffled over to make room for her to sit on the bench. An Elder to her right turned to Annona, setting her hand on Annona's Marking. Annona placed her hand on the Elder's chest, the word Planter etched into her leathered skin, withered and frayed.

"Another week of harvest, and another week of planting completed," Akim said, smiling as he rose to his feet. The Planters and Harvesters hushed, their attention drawn to him.

"And now, on the eve of Selah, we come together to bask in the glory of the Artist's good work, that He so gracefully allows us to participate in. We pause to reflect our gratitude, and to share with one another in the boundless joy," Akim said, taking his cup into his right hand.

"But first, we must reflect on the sacrifice of the Potter, what He surrendered so we might live, and live life to the fullest." Akim's eyes fell on Annona, his eyes squinting revealing the wrinkles layered on his face. Annona looked at his Marking, noticing the faded appearance. Her eyes scanned the other Markings around her. All the Elder's Markings were severely worn, and some could hardly be seen. In contrast, Jore's Marking, along with the others who had been there for a lesser number of seasons, was still distinguishable and not yet worn by sun and sweat.

Jore joined the other workers and poured small amounts of wine into the chalices of the Elder's, followed by pouring the liquid into the cups of the Marked. Reaching for the baskets and cutting boards that held the bread, they each tore pieces from the loaf so that in one hand they held the wine and in the other the bread. Akim waited as each member around the table displayed both of the elements.

"Taste and see that the Artist is good." Akim raised the bread to his mouth, then bowing his head he chewed the bread. The Marked echoed after him, placing the bread in their mouths. It was slightly stale, hardened from sitting on the counter. Annona chewed on the bread, reflecting on her life in Desert's Stone.

Akim brought the chalice to his lips, tipping the cup to release a small sip. The Marked followed, the dry wine washing down the bread. Annona whispered a prayer of gratitude to the Artist. Akim paused as he allowed those assembled around the table to breathe in the quietness.

Annona took in a deep breath as she closed her eyes. She inhaled the aroma of the fermented grapes from the wine, the dough of the bread, the sweat from her shirt, the tang of the cheese spread laid out, and the sweetness of the fruit that had been set in front of her. She peaked her eyes open, scanning the Marked around the table. Eyes were closed, some mumbled words of gratitude while others bowed their head in silence. She kept her head bowed as she raised her eyes to gaze at Akim. A tear had escaped from his closed eyes; he used the back of his palm to wipe it away.

She looked at those surrounding her: the twenty individuals who started as strangers, but quickly, deeply grew to be her family in the Land of Rolling Hills. Through their wisdom and love, the community had become Annona's sounding board when she needed guidance; comforting her when her Aunt had passed and caring for her needs when she lacked anything. Her support system, her care, her family. She never would have imagined finding such great friendships amongst the Marked, especially in a foreign land.

Annona returned her gaze to her lap, hands folded in front of her. *Thank you, Artist. Thank you for my Marking, for my work, for those of the Marked that I sit with, and for this land. Bless them. I taste and see You are good.* Annona rested in the presence of the peace and tranquility. *I don't think it gets any better than this*, she thought to herself.

Slowly, Akim's voice began, his hands raised open above his head, "We thank You, Artist, for what you have given to us. We thank You for allowing us every single day to contribute to work that is so much greater than what we alone can offer. Thank You for giving us the opportunity to pursue what our hands, our heart, and our mind give itself naturally to. We come now to pause and reflect in Your glory. And, with that declared, so be it," Akim said with authority, his eyes opening as he grinned.

Annona grinned as Jore turned and smiled at her, his eyes forming the crescent moons.

"Let's eat," Akim said as he sat himself down, reaching for a bowl to pass to the Marked on his right.

Annona took from the dishes and platters, creating a colourful plate of food to eat. She munched on fruit, while listening to the conversations that took place around her.

One of the unspoken rules while breaking bread was to rest from the discussions of the fields, harvesting, and planting. Breaking bread together provided an opportunity to check the pulse of the team. Conversations involved sharing their emotions, learning about what was going on in each other's home lands, and laughing together in the lightness. Continually focusing on the heaviness of challenges was burdensome. Working in an impoverished land brought a constant feeling of heaviness to the heart. To see children and the crowd suffering, starving, and lacking in basic needs was tragic. At first, Annona had a difficult time not letting it overwhelm her, but, when she was forced to view it every day, she found a way to break through the darkness and into the light. It didn't mean that she neglected to see the suffering or chose to become numb to their pain, but instead had learned through the wisdom of the Elders: focus on the individual the Artist placed in front of her.

Countless times Annona witnessed Akim—so well known and regarded among the crowd—when approached by dozens of those in need, simply lay hands on one. With his full attention he would offer prayer, and if it was within his means, would help the individual in obtaining their need. Annona tried her best to model this behaviour, but found it hard to turn away those who were asking for basic needs.

"Could you pass the salt?" asked Jore.

Annona reached to her right, passing it over.

"Today, news arrived from a Gallery in the Land of Four Seasons. They plan to send us a team of those who have not yet been Marked, still in the discovery of their Relics," Manasses, one of the Harvesters, said. He was sitting across from Jore.

"That's great news! When do they arrive?" Jore asked.

Annona nudged Jore, "We're not supposed to be talking about the fields."

Jore gave Annona a sheepish expression. He clenched his jaws, returning his attention back to Manasses.

"Next week. But, they'll be spending a lot of time in Desert's Stone, specifically with those in need."

Jore shoved a piece of bread into his mouth, speaking through his mouth full of food. "That's good. That'll be an eye opener for them, no doubt."

Manasses nodded his head enthusiastically. "Yeah, for a number of them it'll be the first time they've ever seen poverty."

Jore slowed his chewing, darting his eyes from Manasses back to his plate. His face tightened under the candle-lit table. "Poverty is evident in every land. Perhaps the degree of poverty is not identical, but poverty is relative to each land. We choose what we want to see."

Annona turned her head back to her plate of food, thinking about

Jore's words. In the Land of Four Seasons, she too had seen poverty in Guardian's Ridge. It wasn't of the scale or as evident as it was here in the Land of Rolling Hills.

"True," Manasses agreed. He took a sip from his cup, clearing his throat. "Hey, did I mention my sister is expecting again?"

The table rose with cheers as Manasses shared details about his excitement. Annona listened, laughed, and partook in the surrounding conversation. She ate until her belly was full and her thirst was quenched. Throughout the night she continued to thank the Artist for the family she had stumbled upon: community He had provided her with.

In the late hours of the evening, Akim blessed them before they left for their homes, sending them with joy, peace, and baskets of leftovers from the spread.

16

ROSHGEPHEN

Annona's day of Selah was restless. Thoughts of the weeds affixed to the vegetation caused her feelings of anxiety. Angō made itself comfortable, latching itself to its familiar place on her feet and head. She longed to return to work, wanting to solve the mystery of the weed. Twice she had put her boots on, convincing herself a quick check wouldn't hurt. But, she talked herself out of it, reminding herself it was Selah and that the Elders would not be happy if they found her working on a day of rest.

On the dawn of the work day, Annona rose quickly from a fitful night's rest. She rushed out the door, jogging back to the row she had left on the eve of Selah, reviewing the same plants where she had initially discovered the weeds. She pulled back the leaves to reveal where the stem entered into the earth.

To her surprise, the weed had returned, its head sprouting up from the dirt. Annona shifted back, her mind paralyzed with fear. *What is this?* She asked herself, pulling the weed from the vegetation.

Maybe I didn't pull the weed from this plant. I'm in the wrong row. She bounced to her feet, dashing to the signage at the beginning of the row to make sure she was in the correct field. She was. Annona checked the plant next to it, thinking maybe this one would be without the weed, as she had just pulled it out only two days prior.

Annona slowly drew the leaf back, viewing the stem. The weed was there, attached to the vegetation, interlaced with its stem.

Roshgephen

Annona's heart sank. She tore the weed out, carrying the stubborn weed in the palm of her hand.

"I need to show an Elder," she said aloud as she rose to her feet, searching between the rows to find an Elder. "What have I done?"

"Annona, there you are." Jore jogged up from behind her, his forehead was covered in a slick layer of sweat. His face looked alarmed and panicked, Annona sensed the anxiety strengthen in her chest.

"This is not good," Jore said, panting for breath as he took out the weed that Annona had given him on the eve of Selah. "As soon as I entered the fields today, I raced to the archives room in the warehouse, to see if I could find any literature or reference to the wild plant." Jore was still out of breath, but he straightened himself as he presented the weed to Annona.

"Its distinction is the three leaves and the twisted root. I started by looking through our literature on vines, seeing as that is what it most resembles. However, I couldn't find any vines that had three leaves. I switched to the files of weeds and found one which described the one you uprooted. It was cross-referenced to another cabinet, the folders that are labelled 'Poisonous'".

Annona's stomach did another loop. Her mouth turned dry.

"When I opened the file, there was an astonishing amount of research on the weed. But, it's not just a weed that suffocates after being extracted. An underlining root that festers within the ground breaks off, enriching the soil for the weed to regrow. The regrowth becomes rampant when wheat and barley are grown in close proximity to one another. The nutrients they produce in the ground supplement the weed, causing the weed to grow alarmingly fast. If the fields are not checked, the weeds can spread so rapidly that once it starts, it is impossible to stop."

Annona almost collapsed to her knees as if the ground had disappeared below her. She was the one who had suggested that they grow the barley and wheat close to one another. When Annona had first arrived to the Land of Four Seasons, after she sorted through the vegetation that was invaded and overgrown by common weeds, she had the Planters make new rows of seeds, experimenting with the wheat and barley to see if it would produce a greater yield.

For several seasons it developed rapidly, and the yield had been greater than each season before. However, what she did not account for was the enrichment of the soil: it was becoming perfected with the nutrients needed for the poisonous weeds.

Annona swallowed, but nothing was there. "Can we gather the barley and wheat that is ready to be extracted—or try removing the weed from the stalks until it is ready for harvest?"

Jore shook his head. "It causes the wheat and barley to be inedible, poisoning the roots and infecting the rest of the plant."

Annona's mouth dropped. She turned and looked at the countless fields that surrounded her, all planted with the wheat and barley.

"You're telling me that I've destroyed all of this?"

Fields wasted under a cloudy sky

Jore scratched the side of his temple and exhaled air from his nose. "We need to find the Elders, they need to know."

Jore headed back to the dirt pathway that led to the other fields. Annona stood for a minute, her eyes continuing to scan over the fields. "The yield can't be wasted, this would feed Desert's Stone for the next six moon cycles."

She swung back to Jore, walking in his wake. Jore was silent; the worry was all over his face. The frustration he bore, most prominent in his eyes, un-rattled Annona. Her stomach churned, the shock-waves of Angō ripped through her body as it laid its wires and cables on her.

Within a few minutes they found one of the Elders. Jore spoke, his voice calm, contradicting the erratic and angered expression on his face. He drew the weed from his pocket for the Elder to view. The Elder's eyes expanded like saucers. She shook her head.

"Show me," she demanded. Jore pointed behind him as he hastily turned back the way they just came.

Jore and the Elder went back on the pathway to the infected fields. Annona stood, powerless to move her legs. She shook with fear, regret, and shame. This is my fault, she told herself. *How could I have been so careless?*

Numb, she didn't know what to do. Taking a few steps forward she followed after them, then stopped.

Artist, please do something! She wept, swallowing from her dry throat. Elders ran past her, almost knocking her over as they hurried along the pathway to the wheat and barley fields. A few moments later Akim arrived, limping past Annona as he lagged behind the others. He abruptly paused when he passed Annona, standing still before he shifted himself around.

Akim looked at Annona with a face of sadness and regret as he stumbled towards her.

He settled his hand on her shoulder and looked deep into her eyes. "Annona, sometimes mistakes happen." He gave her shoulder a squeeze. Annona couldn't raise her eyes to his. He changed his weight to his healthy leg, leaning on Annona's shoulder for support. "The biggest mistake I made on the field almost cost me my ability to walk."

Annona raised her eyes to his. Annona took in the deep crevices of his wrinkles, the sun spots on his forehead and cheeks, and the curved scar below his ear.

"In my recklessness and lack of experience I assumed I could pick up the sacks of seeds by myself, even carrying two at a time." Akim snorted and shook his head; his mind's eye was presenting him images that Annona could not see, but she imagined. The bags were difficult to carry, and on her first day in the fields they instructed her not to carry the sacks on her own as it required two workers to lift one sack.

The thought of bearing one sack on your own would have been next to impossible. Two would have been reckless.

"The Elders cautioned me to ask for help, but I assumed I knew better, that I was stronger. In the beginning there was no pain, merely stress in my knee when I carried the sacks. But, as I did things my way, I did not comprehend I was tearing the muscles and ligaments in my legs. One day I went to lift a sack and felt a crack in my knee—the pain so severe it caused me to pass out. I woke up, unable to feel my toes. It took several moon cycles of rehabilitation before I could walk on my own, and to this day I can't move anything heavier than a cylinder brick. My physical deficits remind me every day of my mistakes. I will forever walk with a limp because I thought I knew better than the wisdom of the Elders."

Annona felt a tear slip down her cheek, her eyes quickly refilling.

"Even so, I make a decision each day to identify myself not with my limp, but who the Artist says I am, for the Marking across my—"

"Akim! I'm sorry, but your mistake affected you only. My error prevents thousands of the crowd from getting the food they need!" Annona cried, distressed and undone.

He sighed deeply as he dropped his arm to his side. "You can either give up, or consider this a place of discovery and grace. Only you can make that choice." Akim placed his hand on her Marking for a moment then headed after the others.

Annona stood in her shame, shaking her head. She wanted to follow the Elders, but was terrified to learn the severity of her mistake. As she stood, a sudden weight settled on her back, a hook grasped her leg. It was the Brothers. Annona closed her eyes: she had sensed their approach for a while now, as this would be something she would have to endure through emotionally, spiritually, and physically.

Begrudgingly, she made her way towards the fields of wheat and barley, her mind racing with ten-thousand thoughts of anxiousness and failure, her feet trudging beneath her. Halfway there, the group of Elders and Jore came out from the passage that led to the infected fields. As Annona approached them, she set her sight to the ground in front of her, too ashamed to read their faces, not wanting to see the anger expressed in their eyes.

When she was within speaking distance with them, she raised her eyes. The demeanour of the Elders was calm, some appearing concerned, but to her surprise none showed anger or irritation.

Akim's jaw tensed and loosened. Annona knew the news was not going to be good. He spoke first, his voice calm as he had spoken to her before. "We know the weed as Roshgephen. It's native to the Land of Rolling Hills. Like an airborne virus, it travels rampantly when the harvest is not checked often, or when the soil is augmented with the minerals needed for it to thrive."

Annona shook her head, knowing she was liable for both of the necessities that Roshgephen needed to flourish.

"Unfortunately, any vegetation that comes in contact with Roshgephen becomes affected, and upon consumption can hurt the crowd gravely. We cannot salvage it. The fields need to be extracted and burned. The fields must rest for several seasons until the soil no longer bears the minerals needed for the weed to survive on."

A wave of movement rippled through the Elders, as if simultaneously they felt the burden of the mistake.

Annona couldn't do anything but shake her head. Words refused to come to her voice, but she forced herself to speak.

"I am so, so sorry," Annona whispered, her eyes searching the faces of the Elders. She delved further into her lungs, recovering her voice. "I was so careless, I should have made a point of checking those fields more routinely."

The Elders nodded their heads, some voiced their appreciation for her owning her mistake, while others advised her to not let her mistake overwhelm her.

Annona wanted condemnation. She wanted someone to tell her she messed up. She wanted someone to yell at her and point out how she just destroyed the lives of hundreds of the crowd. But, not one would accuse nor ridicule her. Annona had seen this shared reaction of grace demonstrated before as others in the past had made mistakes in the fields. The Elders were quick to remember mistakes they too had made in their beginnings, and they refused to tear down one who had done the same.

Annona looked at them with a newfound respect and admiration, noting that one day, if she found herself in a similar position, one in which she could grant condemnation or grace, she would aspire to extend grace.

"I can gather half of the Harvesters and Planters to come extract the wheat and barley fields," Jore said, looking to the Elders.

Akim nodded his head in agreement. "Yes, and please let them know all of us need to direct our focus on extraction and burning for the next several weeks. Keep only two or three Harvesters to supervise the healthy yields."

Jore nodded his head and glanced at Annona with a flat expression as he dashed towards the other fields. Annona shook her head again in disbelief, so engulfed by the burden of work she provoked.

"I'll start extracting," Annona said, pivoting to walk around the Elders.

"Wait a moment, Annona." Akim stepped towards her, his eyes full of compassion. He clenched his jaw, revealing his sharpened cheekbones. He took one hand and placed it over her Marking, and with his other hand he rested it on her shoulder. "Again, you have two options. You can bury yourself in guilt and shame with this error. You may want to self condemn or ruminate on what you should have done. Yet, you will not find any condemnation or judgment from us." Several of the Elders nodded their heads in agreement.

"The other choice is a pool of grace that you must jump into, like leaping off of a cliff into the abyss. The waters of grace will surround you and mercy will raise you back to life. You will propel into an entire new awareness of grace and truth," Akim said as the Elders behind him agreed by nodding their heads, some saying, "So be it."

"I hope you choose the latter."

Annona knew in that moment, she was forced to choose between the decision of permitting herself to make mistakes and to grow from them, or the decision of self pity and shame.

Annona lifted her head to meet his eyes, nodding in understanding. It was in moments like this one when she sensed the Painter: in the gentle whispers of grace, the reassuring words of encouragement, the peace that transcended in times of despair.

Akim released his hand. The Elders smiled and nodded, heading towards the weed infested fields.

Annona took her own hand, setting it over her Marking.

"I choose grace," she whispered, following behind the Elders.

Part III

The Labourers Few

"When he saw the crowds, he had compassion for them, because they were harassed and helpless, like sheep without a shepherd. Then he said to his disciples, "The harvest is plentiful, but the labourers are few; therefore pray earnestly to the Lord of the harvest to send out labourers into his harvest."

Matthew 9:36-38

17

MASTER OF DECEPTION

Time passed since the death of Annona's Aunt and the discovery of the weed. Annona continued working the harvest; her daily schedule kept her hands and mind active. She resolved that it wasn't the right time to return to the Land of Four Seasons to be with her family. The grief of her Aunt had subsided as well, due to the continuous need in front of her. The Season of Tears had come and gone and the Land of Rolling Hills returned to ruthless heat.

Extraction of the harvest was well underway. The Marked and Elders cultivated a notable return at the end of the season. The final result of the yield had tripled compared to the season before. As the fields were being reaped, the Planters prepared for the laying of new seeds.

As for the wheat and barley, it was one of the poorest productions ever gathered. The Roshgephen weed destroyed their entire harvest, leaving little to offer Desert's Stone.

Many of the Marked paused in the projects they performed and aided in the eradicating and burning of the Roshgephen weed. The task took several moon cycles to complete. Fields were left desolate, forbidden to be replanted for the next several seasons.

Annona had caused a substantial disturbance amongst the crowd of Desert's Stone and her team. Fighting against her pride, she concluded it was futile to try to make up for her mistake. She worked hard to be diligent in whatever tasks given to her. The Elders continued to demonstrate grace, modelling the way of mercy.

Even with the turmoil produced by the Roshgephen weed, Annona remained confident she was where the Artist wanted her to be. She had completed just over five rotations around the sun in Desert's Stone, offering her life to the production of the harvest. Missing the Land of Four Seasons was inevitable, but her love of pursuing her Marking outweighed the longing for her homeland. She had given her hands, her heart, and her mind to serving the Artist—nothing held a candle to it.

Reflecting on her Masterpiece, an image had been erupting from the centre of the canvas, but it was not yet clear. A framework of an oval, speckled with greens and blues, expanded itself across the canvas. Some nights while lying in bed she would gaze at the splatter of colours and wonder what the finished work would reveal. Before she could ever determine what the finished image would be, she'd unwillingly drift asleep, and her pondering left her without an answer.

As Annona continued to work each day, she never thought to take pictures of her work or of Desert's Stone. No one takes pictures of their home or the places they frequent. Pictures are only needed to revisit a rare moment—prompting a memory no longer tangible. She never considered capturing pictures of the fields mid-harvest. It never occurred to her to snap photographs of the Marked with whom she served alongside. She concluded that for the rest of her existence she would be harvesting. She would continue her duties until she was physically unable, and, when she could no longer, she would pass down her knowledge to the new Harvesters who would take her place. Why would she need pictures or mementos? She required no reminding; she lived her dream and would continue to do so for as long as she could.

Accomplishing what your hands, your heart, and your mind gives itself naturally to does not seem like mechanical, meaningless, boring work. The experience is like breathing. It is pure; takes no thought or adapting; it comes as easily as inhaling air and expelling it out through your nostrils.

Although she experienced hard times, days that seemed long, and distances that felt like chasms… the conclusion remained the same: it was absolutely, without doubt, worth any suffering, any kind of longing, and any call to sacrifice.

To serve with others who followed their Marking was like working alongside an extension of oneself. There were no secret agendas, no personal gain, and no selfish aspirations. Their team relied heavily on all members to use their gifting for the sake of the betterment of others. Everything they established with their hands, heart, and mind was through the perspective of the Artist—to contribute peace, hope, and love to the village of Desert's Stone, to witness oppression be defeated and hope reinstated. They longed to see the crowd have their needs met, to know each child was nourished and loved, and to discover the widow honoured and cared for.

Thus, when it all began to crumble, it fell apart recklessly and without warning. Her world began to shred into a million, unrepairable pieces. Annona was oblivious that the foundation she stood on was wavering, her life about to make a drastic shift. The beginning of the end to giving her hands, her heart, and her mind to her calling had come.

It wasn't truly arbitrary that her dream began tearing at the seams. It started a few weeks back, with a Planter who perceived he was unappreciated. He then conversed with other Planters and Harvesters about his woes, which contributed to a silent rebellion among the team.

In the invisible realm an inevitable chain of events was already underway. Each event like a domino: one falling, toppling onto the other, causing them all to tumble. Abandonment, betrayal, failure, lack of trust, burnout. The final domino would tip Annona in favour of leaving her Marking: no longer desiring to give her hands, her heart, and her mind to the betterment of others.

Actually, it didn't take much for it all to fall apart, but when you are unprepared for the attacks of the opposition, breakdown is inescapable.

Mirmah was the Master of Deception. Mirmah, like Perispaó, appeared to be pleasant on first impression. Sharp, almond eyes sat deep in its skull, leading to a pointed, narrow nose. Its jawline sharp and sunken, lips thin. Its black and white hair was slicked to the back of its neck. It was tall: shoulders a head or two higher than most of the crowd. Mirmah took pride of the prestigious uniform it wore, fashioned with medals of its successes. It was adamant in wiping away any specks of dirt that landed on its jacket or pants, adjusting its medals so they were precisely aligned with one another.

After it successfully deceived its victims, its face would mutate to a mangled mess, revealing its true form. Its eyes turned lopsided and drooped from below the sockets, exposing pink, fleshy skin. A once pointed nose was now crooked and out of joint, and its mouth lost its firmness, dangling from the left side of its lip. Mirmah's arms and legs would shrivel into its shoulders and torso, powerless to further conceal that it truly possessed no limbs, and had to slither to get around.

Mirmah wore a bronze chain around its neck that contained a vile of poison. It carried the poison with it wherever it would go, keeping the vile tucked into its uniform. Mirmah did not need to poison the whole crowd, just one would suffice. A single drop of poison can spoil an entire jar of milk, and so it was with Mirmah's poison. One drop of the potent serum could spread like a rampant disease: able to wipe out any vitamins the milk once had.

It merely needed to deposit one drop of its serum into a mouth of the Marked: one who supposed he wasn't receiving enough praise for his accomplishments, who wasn't rising high enough in the Elder roles, and who felt like his gifting and influence wasn't returning enough victories. Mirmah would attack the worker entrenched in self pity, and the worker—of his own will—would use his tongue to grumble and groan about his lack of recognition. Words of frustration and resentment would spew from the Marked's mouth, uprooting similar feelings of resentfulness in others. Self pity pulled blinders over their eyes, causing them to forget to praise and thank the Artist for what He was entrusting them with. A sick tribe of woeful workers would bear each other's pain and nurse their own, causing dissension amongst the Marked. One drop of poison was powerful enough to eliminate as many as half of the Marked from their work.

Another telltale feature of Mirmah was its stench of sour milk. It could be a hundred metres away, and yet the discerning nose of the Elder knew it was lurking amongst the shadows. Even though Mirmah made itself difficult to see, its odour always gave it away.

Mirmah had come and poisoned one of the Marked. The Planter spread the disgruntled disease to the others, producing doubt, fear, chaos, paranoia, and jealously. No longer did the Marked see themselves working towards a fruitful cause, or preparing themselves against Mirmah's attacks by speaking to and trusting in the Artist. On the contrary, they grumbled, doubting in the guidance provided by the Elders, and felt jealousy of the capabilities or praise that others displayed and received. Their trust was placed in their own strength, in their own feelings, and in their own knowledge.

Mirmah hosted frequent visitations with the Planter. The initial point of contact between the Planter and Mirmah was done in secrecy. Those gifted with discernment felt a shift in the air—they knew something was awry. Within hours of the initial meeting the residue seeped to the rest of the disgruntled. Poison ensued.

18

TUMBLING TOWERS OF BURNOUT

Annona arrived to the fields that morning, clueless about the havoc that Mirmah had unleashed. When she entered the tool shed that morning, the coffee pot was full, untouched. Tools remained hung on the walls, boots perfectly lined the floor. She considered it odd, but figured the other Planters and Harvesters were arriving late. It wasn't until an hour later, after searching over the fields, that she realized over half of the workers were gone. The majority of the Planters had disappeared without notice and several Harvesters were missing too. A functioning team of Planters and Harvesters took many seasons to achieve, but with a single drop of Mirmah's poison it had all fallen apart.

Unknowingly to Annona, this act of abandonment would be the first domino to fall—a series of chain reactions—tumbling from the winds of ruin. The destructive events that would lead her to give up her Marking had begun.

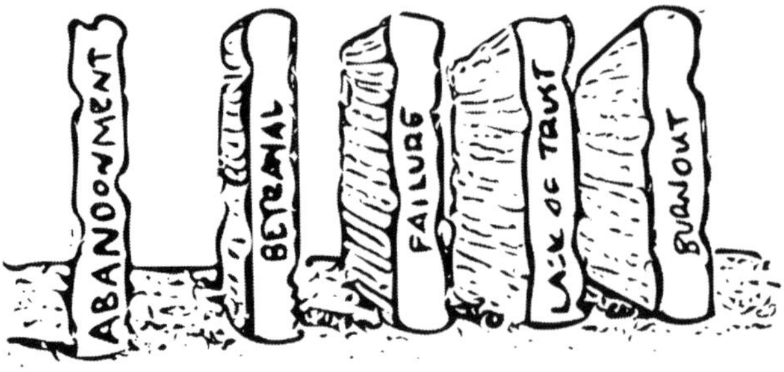

Annona dropped her tool, searching for Jore, who she knew would have answers. She ran back to the toolshed, threw open the doors, entering the small lounging room where he always had his morning cup of coffee before beginning to plant, but he wasn't there. With her anxiety caught in her throat she turned on her heels, quickly exiting the toolshed. She looked over the fields, her eyes scanning for his familiar shape, but she couldn't find him.

Jore was among the missing.

Snapping her head to the left and right, Annona looked for someone, anyone. Between the rows she saw Manasses, sitting in the dirt.

"Where are they?" Annona asked, approaching Manasses the Harvester. He sat in the dirt, pulling at the weeds within his grasp and tossed them carelessly into the air. His plow laid tossed beside him.

"They're gone," Manasses replied as he picked up a handful of earth, sifting the dust into his other hand. "I overheard them talking the other day about quitting, I didn't realize they were serious."

"What did they say?" Annona asked frantically, feeling her throat constrict.

Manasses took a deep breath before responding, his eyes grew into saucers. "They're tired. Sick of performing the same motions each day to reap such limited improvement. The crowd *barely* survive without the nutrients they need, *just* scraping by, and unable to get ahead. Even though the production has been bountiful this season—ample enough to hand out to the crowd twice over—our team cannot get the harvest to them. The majority of the vegetation will be spoiled before its harvested. They lost heart."

Annona bit her lip, her head dizzy as she stood speechless. She understood the frustration. Vegetation would go to waste while outside the door to her home the crowds would remain in desperate need.

"I understand, but to give up altogether! How will this solve anything? Our work has just doubled, now even fewer will receive—"

"It's not only that!" Manasses cut her off, throwing the dirt in his hands to the ground. "We never get recognized for what we accomplish, we slave away for a Marking, and no one thanks us!"

"But, we aren't—"

Manasses jumped to his feet as he slapped the soil from his hands. The abruptness caused Annona to stop speaking. He snatched his plow, his eyes fell on Annona, searching hers. He broke eye-contact with her, sighing as he shifted his stare to the fields. "We have a thankless, life-consuming responsibility. Maybe they're right, perhaps it's time to go."

Annona looked him over, stinging tears brimmed her eyes.

"Where is Jore?" She whispered.

Manasses tilted his head, his eyes squinting as they closed in on her. "Where have you been?" He scoffed. "He's the one who started all of this."

The domino of abandonment crashes as the winds of ruin blow, it shatters into the domino of betrayal.

Annona's mouth dropped, her heart echoed the shock. How was she so clueless to the betrayal taking place? For the past several moon cycles her friendship with Jore seemed off, but she assumed it was because of the mistake she made with the weed. Maybe he needed space. She suspected he needed distance to work out what happened, and she trusted things would return back to normal in time. Jore was instrumental in the eradication of the Roshgephen weed, requested by Akim to interrupt his projects to clear up the issue. He did the job with diligence, never complaining to her about her mistake or the duty to clean it up. She thought he was tired. She thought he was agitated. But, she never thought this could happen.

"I'm finished, this is too much for me. I did my best and I'm ready to do something easier. You should do the same. The harvest is over." He dropped his plow, shook the dust from his shoes, and headed back toward the road.

Annona watched as he strode away, disappearing into a black speck on the road. She envisioned herself following behind him, daring to call it for what it was.

When she looked at Manasses a final time, she noticed a small smudge growing on the horizon. She stood, watching for several minutes, until she was able to make out the figure: Kachash. It came with a smug appearance, chuckling as it dragged itself up to her, oozing a puddle of tar where it settled. Beside Kachash bounced the Brothers, and Angō to its other side, all charged with the static fluttering within its radius.

Kachash clucked the roof of its mouth with its tongue. "This doesn't seem good," Kachash said, eyes twinkling with delight. Picking up the plow that Manasses left, its tar spilled out onto the handle. It feasted its eyes on the lack of workers in the fields. "You've lost over half of your workers. Your fields need someone to move behind you and distribute new seeds. Who will manage that?"

Angō, swaying back and forth, glared at Annona, readying itself to fix its cables and wires on her.

Annona's eyes filled with tears, her heart breaking as the edges of the wound hardened with anger. Kachash was right, who would help their diminished team now? The fields needed planting and harvesting, but not enough of the Marked stood present.

She turned her back to them and faced the fields. An abundance of vegetation—so much good already cultivated—waited to be harvested and distributed to the crowd.

As her eyes skimmed over the land, several of the Elder Harvesters and Planters made their way into the fields. Over their shoulders they brought their tools. They planted and plucked, working as if nothing had changed. The Elders—the heavy lifters, the unshakeable, the Lifers. They were the Marked who would be present through the turns of seasons, changes of workers, the visitation of the Brothers, and the attacks of Mirmah. Experienced in depending on the Artist's perspective and not their own, they were the elite group of the Marked that Annona strived to be part of. Their abiding faith inspired Annona as she watched them bending and harvesting. "Until He calls me home, Kachash, I will not leave this place," Annona said, her back to them all. She wiped off the sludge that had sprinkled onto her arms and legs. When she turned around, Kachash shook its tarred head and slugged back towards the road. Angō, trailed a few steps behind it. The Brothers stayed, lingering, attaching themselves to Annona's back and legs.

The second domino of betrayal cracks into the third domino of failure, her foundation rumbles with confusion.

With so many workers gone, the work doubled for their team. Annona no longer concentrated entirely on harvesting, she also assisted in planting. She could not sow as quickly as the Planters. She stumbled, her hands clumsy when planting the small seeds into the earth. In the past, she had observed the ease in which the Planters could withdraw a single seed, a scoop with their shovel would create the specific depth for the seed to be deposited, and instantaneously they would have it buried in the earth and they were on to the next. Before she'd blink, they would have the seed in the ground and covered in soil, the entire process conducted within a few seconds.

Annona took much longer. She sank her fingers in the side pouch, a small purse-like bag that Planters had designed for holding thousands of seeds. Annona scoured the pockets for the right one. If she didn't check the seed, she could accidentally choose a seed from the wrong pocket. After identifying the appropriate seed she scooped a hole into the earth, but the hole would be too shallow, or she might not have left sufficient distance between the new planting and the last. She didn't possess the innate knowledge or strength the Planters had. The Planters that remained showed patience with Annona, teaching her the correct depth or simply redoing the task themselves—after she had invested her entire day attempting to be a Planter. She recognized how much more efficient Planters were at this task, and this only magnified her anger. Frustration grumbled within her as she recognized that the same task took double or triple the amount of time for her.

Day after day, she wondered if more workers would come, keeping a hopeful eye on the road to the field, waiting for backup to relieve them of their burden. But, they didn't show. Only the few remained, overwhelmed with planting and harvesting for Desert's Stone.

The third domino sways, tilting its direction to the fourth domino—lack of trust. The harsh winds of ruin gust through, causing it to fall like an axe to a wooden giant.

Exhausted, Annona would leave the fields in the evening. The eagerness she had once experienced for her work had worn off. Gone were the days of the feeling of accomplishment. A miserable weariness took its place. Burdened. Stressed. It was grinding on her, prohibiting her from being effective to produce anything besides work. She could only offer half of herself to activities she enjoyed for fun. Annona believed it was more essential to preserve her stamina for the field.

On top of the exhaustion, she was angry with Jore. He had taken off without saying goodbye, giving her no explanation as to why he had left. She had trusted him, convinced he was one who would be there until he was old. But, instead, he had abandoned his Marking and in the process took half of their team with him.

And then there was the whole situation—Annona being entirely to blame—with the Roshgephen weed. It constantly gnawed at her mind. Did her failing to spot the weed before it infected the yield lead him to become resentful of his work? Or maybe *her*? Had the failed crop and the energy demanded to correct her mistake cause him to become disheartened, perhaps clouding his vision of his Marking and Masterpiece?

Her exchanges with the Artist were short and raw: pleading for new workers, asking for Him to lighten the burden, urging for a rejuvenation in her hands, her heart, and her mind. The work was taking its toll on her, harvesting stopped feeling natural—rather, it became a vice, a pressure pinned onto her. Her shoulders slumped, as if they were bearing the weight of the Ends of the Earth to provide for the village of Desert's Stone and the Brothers' unyielding weight due to the stress of the shortage of workers.

Annona stopped attending the breaking of bread with the Elders and observing Selah. Instead, she used the day to attend to the fields for several hours, trying to catch up on the accumulating work. The team, especially the Elders, inquired why she was not going to Selah anymore. She thought it was best not to inform them of what she was doing, knowing they would discourage it. But, for Annona, she believed it was vital. In the underbelly of the disaster, she knew she was at fault. She needed to redeem the error, to use her time and efforts to increase production back to the yield they were capable of providing.

The Artist was silent during Annona's questioning. She would look to Him in places where she had found comfort before, and although she would witness the unmistakable traces of Him, she felt ambivalent. Was He angry with her? Was she to blame for the disaster? Annona's truths about the Artist mangled with traces of fear and doubt, as Angō had secured itself on her feet, its wires bound to her head. It had latched itself to her a few weeks after the workers had left and remained with her in every waking moment.

It didn't speak much, but kept reiterating the same line over and over again, "You are not enough and the work is too great... you are not enough, and the work is too great... you are not enough and the work is too great."

In agony and with much hesitation, after a day of stumbling through planting, she had reached her limit. She was naïve enough to assume she didn't have a boundary, a breaking point, where she would scream, "Enough!" Perhaps if she had known that everyone has a point within them that, when crossed over, causes them to give up, she could have prevented hers from being invaded. But, it was too late now. She was exceptionally tired, extremely worn out, and very bitter.

This was the birth of the death.

The final domino tips, quivering back and forth until it can stay upright no longer. The domino of burnout crashes, shattering upon the ground.

It is finished.

19

AN ACT OF ABANDONMENT

She couldn't take it anymore. With too much to be done, she was suffocating in the infinite patterns of Planting and Harvesting. She was tired, alone, and resentful.

With the final domino fallen and all the events that had contributed to her downfall, she welcomed the act of surrendering her Marking.

Annona arranged the confrontation with the Elders. Her mouth was dry, her heart pounding out of her chest. Her feet walked for her, her body operating in auto-pilot. She rattled off the lines she had memorized, having a hard time meeting their eyes. Some Elders showed disappointment, others offered her expressions of empathy. Annona's posture radiated shame.

She never had expected this day would come for her—not even in her wildest imagination would she be the one giving up on her own Marking. This had been her life. Harvesting was her passion, it was what her hands, her heart, and her mind gave itself naturally to. Her Marking gave her purpose and what she believed living a life for the Artist resembled.

To live in the Land of Rolling Hills was what she dreamt about since she was a child; through all the visits of the Brothers, through the journeying of discovering her Relics, and what both pain and joy had brought her to. The fields had provided her with a place for her hands to give naturally to; where she allowed her heart to establish deep roots with the crowd; where her mind had dreamed of harvesting on fields greater than these. How could she abandon all of this? Did she fight hard enough, try hard enough, give hard enough?

She heard herself saying something to the Elders about opportunity, purpose, gratefulness, exhaustion, and burnout.

The Elders nodded their head in sympathy, laid hands on her Marking, then left her for the fields. Akim was the last to approach her, exposing a saddened smile, embracing her while she quietly wept.

"I'm so sorry," Annona muttered.

He rubbed her back, then pulled her away from his chest to look into her eyes. The seriousness and pain in his face was like a blow to her gut. This was a defining moment for Annona. Every one of her senses locked in the experience, desperately clinging to the moment. Her eyes watched as Akim clenched his jaw and released. *I am the problem he is trying to fix*, she thought to herself. Her nose smelled the sour sweat and the earthy scent of mud. Her fingers touched his leathered skin, the dampness of his shirt as it clung to him. The taste of salt hinted on the tip of her tongue from catching her fallen tears. Her ears would hear his voice for the last time, but her mind could recall the exact tone, sound, and words whenever her memory was triggered by one of these senses.

What Annona did not know, was that whenever one of the crowd would clench their jaw, or when she would taste the saltiness of tears, or perhaps when she would feel her own cotton shirt cling to her skin with dampness, it would trigger her memories of this: this moment of overwhelming failure, shame, and defeat.

"Do good, Annona."

He pulled himself away, setting his hand over her Marking for the last time.

Annona turned herself away from him, heading towards the workshop. She went inside as the anxiety and guilt overwhelmed her. She placed her hands on the counter for support.

Annona stood in her humiliation. There was no absolution of the burden. She felt no lighter, nor relief from her duties. She collected her tools and headed back to her home. As she dragged her feet to the village for the last time, she feared she would never again experience what it was like to serve when her hands, her heart, and her mind gave itself naturally to the betterment of others.

Annona allowed her eyes to survey the fields, attempting to capture every detail she could. Wooden giants perched at the boundaries of the fields. Rows were perfectly aligned, some with full plants, while others were sprouting the heads of something new. She inhaled, smelling the earth, the mud, the dirt that she had become accustomed to—the earthy aroma it produced. She observed as the Elders made their way between the rows, extracting and planting. The recent events having done nothing to provoke their foundations to crumble. Her eyes followed along the skyline. The rolling hills. Beautiful, breathtaking, rolling hills. *How can I live anyplace but here?* She watched as the shades of colours faded behind each facade until they disappeared in the horizon.

She turned away, walking along the road. She fought with her conscious as it screamed at her, begging her to turn around, to go back and make it work. But, her exhaustion was stronger; her burnout was overpowering.

Within a few hours she had hastily gathered what she needed to return to the Land of Four Seasons. Her mind was spinning, catching up to the decision she had made. She left out a shirt from her pack, spreading it across her bed. It was a shirt that covered her Marking, something she had never done before. Putting on this shirt meant the start of a new era: one she was unfamiliar with, an era she never thought would come for her. She proudly wore her Marking, for all to see. She was a Harvester. This had defined her.

She looked at the shirt, her fingers tracing over her Marking, touching the surface of the letters. She propelled herself towards the bed, slipped the shirt on, and headed out the door. Her eyes focused straight ahead, not once looking back.

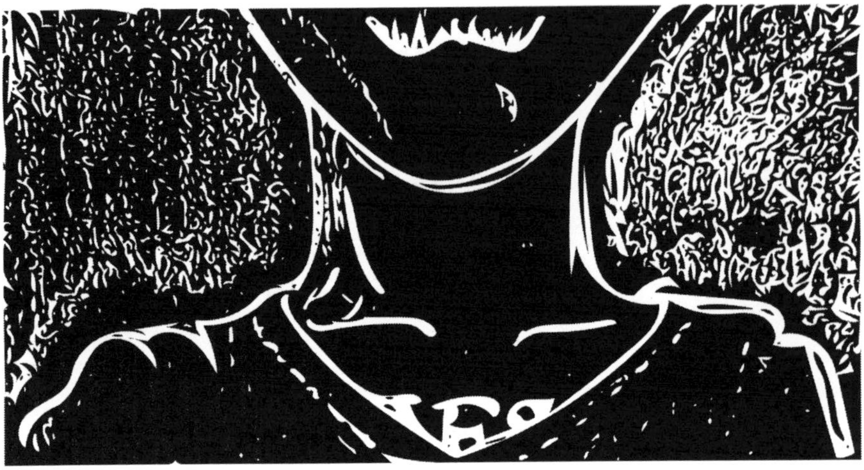

Her Marking, covered.

Part IV

The Anger & the Ache

"But he himself went a day's journey into the wilderness and came and sat down under a broom tree. And he asked that he might die, saying, "It is enough; now, O Lord, take away my life, for I am no better than my fathers."

1 Kings 19:4

20

DESPAIR

Annona startled, waking abruptly to the sound of the crowd as they passed by her bedroom window. She rolled herself over to check the dial hands of the clock revealing it was too early to rise.

She twisted her body back to the position she had been lying in before, not yet fully awake but also not submerged in the trance of deep sleep. Instead, she settled in between the fog of the two worlds, struggling to recall what she had been dreaming of before. The images extended to her mind's eye—visions of faded mountains, running with ease through the hilltops, skies as mysterious as the ocean's blue, a bountiful harvest, and an over abundance of work. Jore stood before her and beamed, he instructed her not to slow down, while behind him an electrical fire storm barrelled forward. Suddenly, his smile turned to fear, he screamed, telling her to run. Blue skies turned to the darkest ocean's black. The clouds swarmed with severe gusts, and the fields caught fire. Hallow. Gaunt. Black. Jore disappeared into a cloud of soot, and she was left alone, standing before the Elders, telling them she's finished. Deserts' Stone wasted away, not a brick stood on top of the other. It all laid in ruins.

Abruptly, Annona forced her eyes open. "It's not real," Annona told herself, shifting to her side. "It's not real." Annona sighed, her heart pounded against her rib cage. She closed her eyes, trying to recall the part of the dream where the harvest was full and the sky was calm.

The beauty of dreaming is that it requires no wealth and disregards your land of origin nor does it care for which papers you hold. Dreams possess no limitations, no borders, and no barriers. Your mind is free to transport you to anywhere and to be anyone. They allow you to stretch across the realms of the earth, within an eight hour cycle, and all without leaving your bed.

The dream ended, fading from Annona's mind. She was sure it would return that night as she had had the same recurring dream for several moon cycles. She pushed herself up, shoving the blankets off her body, her toes touching the cold floor. Her mind's eye still burned with the faded image of the mountains, the winding dirt pathways, and the routes she was running on to reach her destiny.

When she first had returned to Guardian's Ridge, she hardly believed her key would fit back into the slot of her front door. How could it? After five seasons of her life spent abroad, she had changed. Annona wasn't the same anymore. Something had shifted inside of her. Her shell: skin, hair, body—the physical—was similar. But, inside, her character, her soul was different. Perhaps tainted even. Her perspective on life, pain, and purpose was no longer in alignment to what she had once believed. Everything she had understood before vanished the moment she abandoned her Marking.

No longer did she experience joy when she thought about the Land of Rolling Hills. The memories only caused her pain. Her mind longed to reminisce about her time as a Harvester, but she would force the images out of her head, redirecting her attention to her daily tasks. She would never experience harvesting again. Her Marking was finished.

Finding a job at a greenhouse just outside Guardian's Ridge allowed her to use the skills she learned in the Land of Rolling Hills. Tasks were repetitive, slow paced, and predictable. It did not involve critical thinking for Annona, and, compared to the pace she was used to in Desert's Stone, the work came easy to her.

At the day's end she would return to her home, distracting herself with projects around her house, finding tasks to keep her hands busy. If she occupied her hands, she could occupy her thoughts with something beyond her failure. The projects would swallow her thoughts of worry. Hobbies surfaced from when she was much younger, before discovering what her hands, her heart, and her mind gave itself naturally to. They held no purpose beyond personal gratification and required no feeling from her heart; it was what her hands could give themselves naturally to while distracting her from ruminating.

Anything in her home that reminded her of the Land of Rolling Hills had been packed away in boxes or shoved under furniture, hidden from the light. The watch gifted from the Elders she tore off her wrist the moment she had returned to Land of Four Seasons, burying it in the bottom of her satchel. Within the same week that she returned to Guardian's Ridge, she went to the markets and came home with a new watch. Annona justified the new purchase to herself: the old watch triggered too many emotions. She didn't want to be reminded of the harvest each time she saw the faded leather of the band out of the corner of her eye. Feelings of failure weighed on her whenever she became conscious of the presence of the watch on her wrist. The constant ticking her watch produced as the minute hand slowly slid round the face matched the pounding of Annona's heart as she lay restless in bed. No, this watch was nothing but a minefield of emotions: dread, worry, anxiety, and fear. The watch had to be hidden away.

Songs that once were her anthem—the same ones she had sung with conviction and joy on the roads each day to and from the harvest—now brought her pain. Decorations and tools she had acquired as treasures that used to bring her honour had turned into her greatest shame. She buried them under her bed—out of sight and out of mind—all in an attempt to numb her pain.

During her fourth rotation around the sun in Desert's Stone she had a special pair of harvest shears commissioned for the Painter. Asking a local from Desert's Stone to create them for her, he formed the shears with tungsten, the blade black and speckled with rubies, the handles a titanium silver. Annona had hoped that the Painter might find a place for them on His bookshelves of tokens of appreciation. At this point she had no motive to see them nor give them to Him. They now laid in the back of a desk drawer, discarded.

No longer a nagging thought she could shrug off, she now accepted anything she would do from this moment on as meaningless. Her unfinished Masterpiece would remain forever as it was: no more colours and no more definition brought to the blurry shapes. The minute she had returned from the Land of Rolling Hills she knew what she had to do with her Masterpiece. She removed it from her sack, tightly rolling it up, and crammed it into a box. She buried it in the back corner of her closet behind boxes of forgotten memories. The sight of the chaotic disarray of colours, the smeared image that would never transform into the work of art that He meant it to be provoked deep shame in Annona's soul.

Annona told herself she had to do this—the hiding, packing, removing, and controlling—it was all required for her self-preservation. She would not allow herself, not even for a minute, to reminisce about harvesting; she kept her mind wound on a tight leash, restricted and confined. She intentionally kept her mind from drifting to the Land of Rolling Hills, because thinking would progress to feeling, feeling to longing, longing would certainly escalate to pain, and pain would burst wide the dam of the brewing flood of *anger*.

One day bled into the next. Nothing notable, nothing of worth was left on a day. She became accustomed to the new routine: rise, dress, work, return, putter around in meaningless activities, and sleep. She needed nothing more, and desired nothing less.

The solution was not found in Gaurdian's Ridge. No matter how hard she tried to put her energy into other tasks, nothing was like the harvest. It was what the Painter had Marked her to do, and without performing in that task, a blackhole began to form in her heart.

The blackhole.

The erosion within her chest.

The symptoms!

A sudden memory surged to the forefront of her mind, a memory from before her Marking had been given to her, running into Adah on her Marking Day. Adah's warning replayed in her mind, the clarity of her words as if she had been standing before her now. How could she have forgotten about the symptoms? The warning from Adah to not be Markless?

"Anger. Bitterness. Aching. Hopelessness. Denying your Marking always causes the symptoms. Accepting a fake calling does nothing to give hope! The symptoms that rise from denying your Marking pushes you into mental misery. Not pursuing your Marking only worsens the symptoms. You will wander around as if a crater—a black hole—is constantly causing misery within your chest, burrowing into the edges of your heart."

Annona's mouth turned dry, a sinking feeling welled and stormed within her chest.

Do I have the symptoms?

Passion and purpose had once lived in her heart, and, unbeknownst to Annona, had left a signature on it. When she withdrew from the harvest, passion and purpose disappeared. Whether they had left of their own volition or Annona had forced them out, didn't concern her. What remained was a gaping crater, a deep cavity inside her chest, which refused to be filled by the barrenness of what she was producing now.

21

ANGER

Craftsmanship begins with inspiration. Inspiration alone does not grant the gifting, but it must be pursued through dedication, determination, and grind. Potters who create pottery dedicate hundreds of hours to sharpening their skill. The gifting does not start with their hands picking up a lump of clay and throwing it on a kick-wheel. The exercise begins with a spark of interest inspiring the study of the art. Studying leads to dedicating hours upon hours of practice, full of repeated failures and victories, each time learning from their previous mistakes. Until eventually, one day, through both failures and achievements, the potter constructs their magnum opus. A piece that they are so proud of, that shows both the potter and everyone around them the reward of their dedication.

Annona much like the potter had dedicated everything she was to pursuing her Marking. It was her only focus. But, now it was gone. It was as if she had created a beautiful piece of pottery, only to have it ripped away by an intruder, teasing and taunting, who then smashes it into a million pieces before the potter's eyes. As the potter stares at their beloved work, sadness overwhelms them as the truth settles in: the potter will never look at the finality and beauty of that pot again. But for Annona, she has no intruder to blame. She lifts her eyes to the culprit, only to find herself staring into wide, familiar eyes—her own eyes. In this moment the mourning is cast aside and all that is left is hatred paired with a deep fury.

The anger buried within Annona was ferocious; like a lion starved and neglected: its hunger was rampant. The lion—her anger—paced back and forth, craving for the smallest scrap so it could have an excuse to unleash its assault.

Anger

Annona could contain her anger most of the time. It tingled in her fingertips when a reminder of the Rolling Hills came into view. She'd dart her eyes away from viewing the Markings of the crowd. Annona experienced the swelling in her heart when the crowd spoke about their Markings and purpose, invoking her anger and sadness—a force of misery.

Other times it would slip out when someone made a mistake. The starved lion would roar, scratch, and devour the victim. The behaviours that flowed from her anger horrified her. However, Annona recognized the gratification she felt upon unleashing the prowling lion within.

When listening to the crowd discuss topics like life, purpose, Markings, and passions, Annona felt she must leave the room. Subjecting herself to these types of conversations only magnified her failure and guilt. At one point in her life she too would have shared her views and opinions, standing bravely on what she understood to be true. But, Annona could not find that voice any longer: she had silenced it. When invited into conversations about Markings, the taste of disgrace and guilt would erode Annona's tongue. Swallowing the bitter poison, she'd remain quiet. Annona knew *she* was an abandoner. She acknowledged it was *she* who had given up her Marking.

Annona knew, deep in her broken heart, that she was not just the potter, but the intruder who had taken the pot into her own hands and shattered it into a million pieces. This knowledge heightened her anger and own self-contempt. On top of all this, she was tired. She used to explain her point of view, standing on what she supposed was true. But, now, what for? For it all—her dreams, beliefs, efforts, hardships, perseverance, blood, sweat, and tears—had come tumbling down on her like a house of cards.

The anger and pain living in Annona had not been provoked by losing her work—that was replaceable. The misery was due to the failure of her childhood dreams: the aspiration to serve the nations. The dream was dead, and it wasn't supposed to be.

She had faithfully pursued the Marking on her chest. She had allowed the Painter to Mark her. She had found her Relics—she had followed the Artist. She had attended the Gallery, she gave as she was supposed to. Just as she should have, she had followed each and every step, *and in the end it all failed*. What did this mean about her Marking? About the Artist? Could she trust Him anymore? This life, one of aimlessness, was not supposed to be her life! Annona had completely heeded everything the Artist put in front of her.

She recalled dozens of times listening to the visiting Elder Harvesters and Planters who lived in the Land of Heat or Land of Rolling Hills. They would speak at the Gallery to inspire others to join the harvest. And, for Annona, it had done just that. It was from a young age that her curiosity of living in an oppressed land was piqued. This inspiration carried over into her education, causing her to always choose projects that brought awareness to the suffering happening in the nations that were being neglected, exposed, and raided. She had made tough decisions in romantic relationships, not giving her heart even the chance to develop feelings with companions who did not want to follow their Marking, or those whose passions didn't align with hers. These tough decisions led into financial strain and investments, choosing products she knew were ethically sourced. She chose to fund projects from all around the Ends of the Earth that provided the crowd's basic needs. All these decisions had contributed to her Relics, what she would choose and not choose, as she searched for her passions in Lands that needed help.

Leaving the harvest wasn't just a loss of meaningful work for Annona; the loss was of her *entire* identity, everything she had aligned herself with, everything she had believed in.

The hollowness she felt was from the thousands of little decisions she had to make, to the hundreds of actions she had to perform, to the exact moment of determination when she renounced everything she had known and started over in the Land of Rolling Hills. At one stage in her life, back when she was naïve, she would be absorbed in her dreams of the harvest, in the boundless promise that the Artist would use her for something great. However, today, what did she have to set her eyes upon? The dream was behind her: finished and expired.

Kachash's trail left in Annona's bedroom

Kachash left a trail of tar throughout Annona's home. When Annona would wake in the morning and head to the kitchen, the sticky substance would cover Annona's feet. At first Annona would try to scrub it off, but, being so sticky and thick, it required too much effort for her to scrub it off merely to have to repeat the process again the next day. Defeated, she resolved to just allow it. The tar had progressed to her torso, leaving splatters on her arms and hands. Debris, dirt, and scraps blown by the winds stuck to her. She only bothered to pull off the garbage that was noticeable to others, covering the remaining sap with clothing.

Annona would not leave her home without her shirt that concealed her Marking. It resulted in fewer questions asked, keeping her emotions numb and tucked away. The Marking, which she used to show with honour, was now an admonition of her greatest failure.

Sometimes when Annona would run errands in Guardian's Ridge she would bump into an old friend. Her friends would ask her about the harvest, Desert's Stone, or the Land of Rolling Hills. Annona had prepared herself for their questions by memorizing a response. She offered them a statement that would answer their question without scratching the surface of her ache. The response required no fluctuation of emotions from within her.

"How was your time in Land of Rolling Hills? How was the harvest? What was it like?" The questions, simple queries, from family and friends evoked the truth roaring at the back of Annona's throat. The answer—the truth—that Annona wanted to give would undoubtedly result in backfire from her friends.

"I didn't want to leave. I don't want to be here, don't you get it? I'm supposed to be there. That's why it says 'Harvester' across my chest, and not 'Gardener'. This is all a mistake, me being here—I came back too early. This wasn't supposed to happen, not to me at least. I know what my Marking is. I understand what my hands, my heart, and my mind give itself naturally to, and it's not this. I don't know how to fit in here, I don't want to fit in here! I don't know what I'm supposed to do in this land. Nothing I do here seems right. I feel like a fish out of water, like a sailor without a boat, like a traveler without his compass. The Painter Himself gave me this Marking, now I can't get rid of it. This Marking, it's a curse—it constantly reminds me of my defeat." That's what her heart would weep and what she wanted to say, but the answer she'd give would emerge with a confident nod, and went something like: "It was good. I miss it, but grateful to be home."

Annona was terrified of the emotions that would flee wild and rampant out of her if she were to sincerely reflect and identify what she had given up. She was afraid that the emotions would explode from her soul, like a thousand nuclear explosions wounding and killing whoever and whatever existed in its path. Friendships, relationships, intimacy—they didn't stand a chance. The idea of exposing the lions that prowled within terrified her. To imagine someone witnessing the place in her heart that was hallowed and darkening, breaking and tearing—the heart she had become so ashamed of—better it was for her to be in isolation.

To avoid further humiliation, she locked herself away. She would travel solely to the greenhouse and then withdraw directly to her home. Annona isolated herself from her friends, surrounding herself with those who she concluded she could depend on to avoid talk of the harvest. Too distressed to engage in deep conversations, too riddled with guilt to recognize what she left behind, she embraced the superficial, because it was much easier to digest.

Annona used to protect herself from Perispaó, making sure it did not have domination over her life. Now, Annona welcomed it, allowing it to chant its twisted lullaby of distraction. She made sure there were loud tunes that would drown out her reflections as she went to and from the greenhouse. To keep her mind distracted, Annona kept busy with never ending projects at home, playing films in the background, the arbitrary noise keeping her company. Perispaó soothed her pain, smothering her heart's cry to keep it from spilling over.

Since her return home, she had been avoiding the Artist. She wasn't interested in any kind of confrontation. She wasn't sure who would confront who: the Artist, who might ask her what had happened, or Annona herself, if she dared, might demand why *He* had allowed this to happen.

The question that resonated like a war drum inside her chest was why the Artist would give her a Marking she would ultimately fail in. A failure that would hurt her and burn her out so severely that she would lose her devotion to pursue it, feeling so much humiliation she would never again live a life that was meaningful. She did not understand what she had done wrong, why He was silent when she stopped with her hands, her heart, and her mind. She only had hoped to serve the Artist and to help those of the oppressed crowd.

Now, the Marking had nothing to do with her purpose, but served as a constant reminder of her failures.

Her dream was dead.

Life held no purpose.

Everything, from this point forward, was meaningless.

22

ISOLATION

"Annona!"

Her eyes sealed close, her shoulders hunched into her neck, the muscles in her cheeks stiffened. Annona hadn't expected to run into anyone at the markets, and the sound of her name being called from among the crowd was like nails on a chalkboard. She hoped her reaction was subtle enough to not be detected by the onlookers. Before turning around she took a quick breath, relaxing her tightened muscles.

Breathe.

Beside a carton of peaches stood Adah, wide eyed and smiling. Her loose curls hung softly by her cheeks. Her attention darted from the peaches to Annona as she let out a small chuckle before she spoke. "My goodness! We're always running into each other in the most random places!"

"Hello, Adah. Good to see you," Annona said with a smile. She adverted her eyes, not wanting them to reveal the contradiction of her words with how she felt seeing Adah for the first time since returning.

"I heard you had come back." Adah picked up a peach, her fingers sunk into the skin. With Adah's attention on the fruit, Annona let out a small wince. *How much did she know?*

"Yeah, several moon cycles ago."

"Why? If you don't mind me asking?"

Why? Was that judgment in her tone? Annona needed to make a quick decision. She didn't trust many with the truth. Annona thought of her premeditated answers, the ones in which she would address the lack of safety, the demand of the work, and missing her family and friends. They were suitable answers offering pieces of the truth, but not anywhere near the whole truth. She looked at Adah, studying her demeanour. Was she trustworthy? Adah placed the peach back inside the cart, and picked up another. She looked at Annona and gave a smile, returning the peach to the cart, choosing another. This was a friend she believed she could be honest with, her mistakes, betrayal, and burnout. One with whom she could share.

Tell her the truth.

Annona took a deep breath as she felt the drawbridge being lowered—ever so slightly—from the thick, granite walls that guarded her heart.

Five minutes.

That's how long it took for Annona to spill out all she needed to say about leaving the Land of Rolling Hills. She began with guarded walls, saying bits and pieces of what happened. Adah's eyes widened at all the right moments. Adah didn't stop her. She seemed to be receptive, so Annona kept speaking, the words spilled into the atmosphere, impossible to retract. She spoke of Roshgephen, Mirmah, Jore, the Harvesters and Planters leaving, the pain she had caused Akim, and how Desert's Stone was probably deteriorating with the sudden lack of workers. Adah winced and murmured when Annona spoke of the burnout. She shook her head in disbelief when Annona discussed the betrayal. With each sympathetic look and wince, Annona's walls came down, down, down. With her guard lowered, the anger and ache rushed out like a flood. She gave the wounding details in clumps, letting it all hang out for Adah to sort. She didn't hold back. Annona released her pain. The desperation she sensed. She unleashed her anger. Annona stopped after discussing the aching. A silence grew between them as Adah placed a peach inside her basket.

Adah sighed loudly, her head shook in disbelief. "Wow, Annona. I had no clue. I heard you came back, but didn't realize it was that bad."

Annona nodded her head. *Maybe she'll agree to meet with me. Maybe she'll take me under her wing until I sort things out. She understands.*

"But, I'm a bit confused."

Annona paused. "What do you mean?"

Now it was Adah adverting her eyes, taking a sudden interest in the products surrounding them. "Well, it's just that you say you're burned out and that you can't pursue your Marking right now. But, what you don't realize is that it is your purpose. *Of course* you feel an aching within your heart." She stopped looking at the produce around her, taking one of Annona's hands into her own, gently placing her hand on top of Annona's. "I totally understand your anger and hopelessness. You're not living in your purpose, you know?"

Annona forced a dry swallow. Her mind was racing with how to answer Adah. Wasn't what she had just explained enough to understand why she wasn't pursuing her Marking? She didn't want to explain even further—in the middle of a market of all places—why she had left. Why she couldn't pursue her Marking right now? Did she not hear anything she had just said? Before she could summon a response, Adah started again.

"I didn't mean to pry, you know? And I hope you know I'm not trying to tell you what to do with your life. But, what I'm saying is that you're going to keep feeling this way as long as you neglect your Marking. Using our hands, our hearts, and our minds is what gives us purpose. It helps our society and it honours Him. Look at the Potter! He used His hands, His heart, and His mind while serving the crowd!"

Annona gave a small smile, slowly withdrawing her hand.

A mistake.

This was a mistake.

I shouldn't have opened up to her.

I should've stuck to the script.

I must get out, now!

"Right, Adah. Yes, maybe in a few cycles I'll give it another go."

"The sooner the better, Annona. You don't want one bad experience to deter you from following your Marking! I wouldn't even wait that long. It'll only get worse!"

Annona nodded her head. *Make something up! Walk away!*

"You know what I'm talking about"—Adah leaned in closer to Annona, her voice forcibly hushed—"*the symptoms.*"

Annona cut her off, she had heard enough. "Well, I've got some errands to run, it was nice seeing you."

Adah dropped the peach back down in the crate. "Already? Well, it was so good seeing you too, Annona! Let's go for a coffee soon, they opened a new shop in the village!"

"So I heard," Annona said.

Adah searched Annona's t-shirt, her hand half raised, giving Annona a confused smile. Annona realized Adah wanted to place her hand over her Marking before leaving. Annona pointed to where the Marking laid beneath her t-shirt while Adah hesitantly raised her hand. Annona smiled back awkwardly as Adah rested her hand on the hidden Marking, Adah's eyes of concern attempted to search Annona's. She couldn't hold her stare. Adah gave her an empathetic smile, dropped her hand and passed by her.

Walked right into that one. Angō's jolts of anxiety streamed through her, pumping into her system like an IV. Little did Anona know, this conversation would cause her heart to retaliate. For now, she would weep. She would trudge home angrily, feeling cheated, robbed, and foolish for opening up to someone who could not understand. But, after the night of sadness and anxiety had passed, her heart would harden.

Her heart of flesh would build a fortress of stone around her wounds, one taller and thicker than the one she had just broken through to share her story with Adah. A deep vault would erupt from within her, locking her heart away. She wouldn't be so foolish next time, willingly revealing her woundings to someone. No one could understand. She was an island: alone, stranded.

A fortress around her heart

No, Annona wouldn't be meeting Adah for coffee. The *last* thing she would be doing would be meeting with her for a coffee. That was a cup far too bitter, even for her.

23

GUILT

Images of the rolling hills faded from her mind's eye. The dawn's light penetrated through her closed eyelids. She shuffled over again while fluffing her pillow, trying to force herself back to sleep. It was the same recurring dream she had experienced for several moon cycles in a row, tormenting her both when her eyes were closed and even when they were open.

Today was Selah. The time to pause, reflect, and wonder. In the first few moon cycles of being back, she had looked forward to Selah and attending the Gallery. But, as the heaviness of her failures overtook her thoughts, the Gallery became a place that was unpredictable: saturated with anxieties and fear. Erratic and confusing, the Gallery no longer felt safe to Annona. Some weeks she slipped in and out without notice. The Shepherd's words, which were supposed to strike the strings of Annona's heart, instead seemed like personal attacks against her. The talks concentrated on following your Marking, urging members to get off the sidelines and to take action. Lost in how to respond, Annona knew her choices wreaked of selfishness. Annona no longer knew how to engage, knowing her life was touched by failure and burnout; she felt as though she was completely out of commission.

She bent herself over the bed, resting her feet on the cold floor while her heavy head laid in her tired arms.

"Don't go," Angō said, its shock-waves of anxiety pulsated through her body, "Just stay home and relax."

"Perhaps use the day to clean your house, or visit the new coffee shop that opened," Perispaó said, pressing on the knots in her shoulders.

Annona shifted from the side of the bed, her eyes glancing across her room. It needed a good cleaning. Kachash had produced a snail like trail: traces of tar that zig-zagged across the floor.

Annona groaned as she dropped her head into her hands. Her fingers pressed into her closed eyelids until images of light like fireworks burst from behind her eyes. Attending the Gallery would require listening to yet another lecture about Markings, which would further her anxiety and thrust her entire day into a chasm of thoughts of harvesting. However, if she skipped the Gallery and went to a coffee shop it would be painless. Yet, she would wonder what she might miss out on. What if the Shepherd finally spoke about those who pursued their calling and failed? What if he finally shed light on her situation and offered her renewed hope? She needed hope, she was desperate for it.

Reluctantly, she stood to her feet, still undecided as to where to go that morning. She settled on the idea that she would start with breakfast, readying herself for either option.

Without much thought she attended to her hunger. When her mind would drift to the harvest or Markings, she would redirect her awareness to think of something else: her projects, a film she had just watched, or her work.

Annona laid her dishes in the sink, heading back to her room. The same thoughts lingered in her head: *If I go to the coffee shop, I will feel even more guilty for skipping the Gallery. If it becomes too much, I can always leave.*

Annona knew she needed to attend the Gallery—truancy was a dangerous habit to start herself on.

As she dressed, she debated whether to cover her Marking. If she concealed it, it might attract further attention as to why she had it covered. On the other hand, if she didn't cover it and anyone were to see it, they would immediately know she was not pursuing her Marking, for there were no fields to harvest in Guardian's Ridge, nor in any of the surrounding villages.

Annona tilted her head as she inspected the shirt that exposed her Marking, resolving it was best to avoid the temptation to hide anything. She tugged the shirt over her head and glanced at herself in the mirror.

Harvester.

Failure.

A sigh escaped from her lips, pulling her gaze away she headed out the door.

The day was bound to be a beautiful one. The skies were a sea blue and a gentle breeze brushed upon her back, guiding her steps forward. She inhaled the crisp air; the oxygen filling her lungs. Her feet glided along the sidewalk, as she continued walking to the Gallery. *Maybe it will be a good day*, Annona thought to herself as her sight caught two birds in flight overhead. The streets of Guardian's Ridge were calm on Selah. Besides the writers and creators seeking refuge at a coffee shop or a family heading to the Gallery, there was no one else in sight.

Annona was halfway to the Gallery when she realized she had forgotten her Book of Suneidésis. She came to a sudden halt, considering the time it took to return home. Annona looked at her watch, concluding she would have to borrow the Books of Suneidésis the Gallery provided.

She tucked her hands into her pockets as she strode along the sidewalk. Anxious of the subject that the Shepherd might speak about. She repeatedly reminded herself that she could slip out the back if the guilt became overpowering.

Before she realized where she was, the crunching of gravel changed below her feet. She looked up and found she was standing at the entrance of the Alley of the Invisible.

As always, the Alley was dark. Garbage piled on the sides of the pathway. The smell of the trash was overwhelming. Annona covered her nose with her sleeve. Her face scrunched up as she searched for the source, but then quickly thought it was probably best not to find out.

She looked to the right, debating whether to walk the extra three blocks to avoid passing through the Alley. She scanned as far as possible into the dark Alley, not seeing any imminent danger or threat.

Already running late, she concluded she didn't have the time to go the extra three blocks. The thought occurred to her that she'd experience more guilt avoiding the Alley, especially considering that the crowd in its corridors were invisible to so many. *I will not partake in the drowning out of their voices, nor pretend that they are invisible*, she told herself. The voice she resorted to distinguish between black and white spoke to her, the same voice that began her journey into caring for the crowd of the oppressed. Before she had time to administer any self control, she felt angered. *The same voice that tricked me so long ago*, Annona thought. *The voice that started this journey of failure.*

Annona stepped over a torn bag of garbage, placing herself in the mouth of the Alley. The crunch of the gravel scraped against her shoes. She strained her eyes to locate the twisting roots and vines that wished her to stumble.

The Alley had not changed. From the first time she had entered it many rotations ago, no progress had been made. Buildings in Guardian's Ridge had modernized, sidewalks widened, bike lanes were added, wooden giants planted, and roads repaved, yet the Alley had remained untouched. Over countless seasons, the Alley of the Invisible had withstood the grip of time—time bore no grip here. The Alley was ageless: neglected from the moment it was created. She wondered what efforts, if any, were being made to reach the pack who were poor, wounded, and rejected living inside this Sheol. Some stood with their backs to the walls, others stretched out on cardboard mats. Annona passed some talking with each other, while others buried themselves in the darkest corners of the Alley, speaking with forced whispers to those not seen.

A rising sadness erupted in her chest. It was the same feeling she had experienced when entering a village in the Land of Rolling Hills where she could witness how poverty was crippling the children of the crowd.

We choose what we want to see, Jore's words whispered in the back of her mind. Annona's eyes welled with tears. The pace of her breathing accelerated.

Annona kept her sight focused on what was in front of her, stepping over the roots and weeds, darting between piles of trash. Covered in rags and dirt, the crowd hidden within the Alley became overwhelmingly hard for Annona to see. The sight caused palpitations in her chest and a deep ache in her heart. Her breath staggered with shallow inhales. She hadn't prepared herself for the effect of witnessing the suffering. The pain of others seemed non-existent, she had been drowning in her own pain for so long that it had became all-consuming.

Since her return to the Land of Four Seasons, she had refused to involve herself in the suffering and needs of the Ends of the Earth, especially for those in poverty. Her knowledge and awareness had once been the centre of her purpose, but it was too upsetting now, being entrenched in her own guilt. Once she had faith that she could make a difference. But, her failure had shown her otherwise, it was foolish to think she would make any difference at all.

Her gut twisted with guilt, shame, and disappointment. *Why didn't I just go around?* Annona asked herself. *This really proved to be too much.*

Mechanically, she moved herself forward, weaving and darting through the staggered obstacles of the Alley. After a few more bumpy steps, she saw the change in the gravel. The jagged rocks smoothing themselves out into flat concrete, which then transitioned into the cobblestone roads.

Annona gasped in relief as she patted the dirt and dust away that had tracked onto her shoes and pants. Families and couples passed her as they entered the Gallery's entrance. They laughed and grinned, shaking hands as they greeted one another with joyous expressions.

Annona smiled, reminding herself where she was. *It will be good, it will be okay*, she told herself repeatedly as she stepped into the Gallery.

24

CONDEMNATION & SHAME

"Welcome!" A welcomer greeted her at the door. As he enthusiastically shook Annona's hand, he smiled a big toothy grin. Across his chest was the Marking "Supporter." His eyes flashed from her stare to her Marking, then bounced back to Annona's eyes.

If he noticed my Marking, his face didn't show it, she thought.

"Good morning," Annona said, dipping her head as she protectively raised her hand to her Marking, stretching her fingers to cover as much as she could. Annona darted past the welcomer and stepped into the atrium, keeping her eyes on the floor as she made a clear cut to the hall.

"Good morning!"

Another welcomer blocking the entrance to the hall smiled at Annona. Annona smiled back, ducking her head as she approached the hall.

Almost there.

"Morning," Annona said to yet another welcomer positioned at the hall's door.

"Oh, a Harvester!"

Annona raised her line of sight to the welcomer, her eyebrows furrowed. *Why did she have to point it out?* Without realizing, she inhaled sharply, holding her breath. The welcomer saw her discomfort, quickly snapping out of her greeting patterns to explain her remark to her.

"Oh! Don't fret! It will be a fabulous talk for you today!" Patting Annona's back she lightly tugged her into the hall. The welcomer passed a pamphlet to Annona and stepped aside, allowing Annona to pass.

After a beat, she exhaled. "Okay, thanks," Annona answered cooly. Inside, her warning bells of fear were ringing.

I'm sure she's pointing out my Marking because she's trying to be encouraging. She must know I'm not following mine, maybe she thinks after today I will, Annona told herself to soothe the uneasiness growing inside her belly. The warning bells retreated to the back of her mind. She peered into the hall, scanning the empty rows near the back of the room. Finding an empty seat strategically close to the exit doors, she slipped into a chair. She scanned over the pamphlet nervously, without retaining any of the information printed on the glossy paper.

A deep breath filled her lungs as she examined the back of the crowd's heads, her ears adjusting to the volume of the hollow room. Her eyes traced along the supporting arch of the roof, taking in the refinement of the design and modern architecture.

"Good morning and welcome to the Gallery!" The voice of an enthusiastic presenter echoed through the sound system, quieting the crowd's chatter. The focus of the crowd fixated on the member standing centre stage.

The presenter rattled off the events of the Gallery. This included the multiple events planned for the crowd, the invitations for the Marked to become more engaged with their community, and welcoming the crowd who were visiting the Gallery for the first time.

The arches overhead stole Annona's attention. She charted the contrast from the industrial ceiling to the wood spine. The presenter's voice muffled in the back of her mind as she switched from admiring the architecture to staring at the back of the heads of the crowd. She drifted her focus from member to member, wondering what their individual Marking might be. She looked over to the Marked sitting a few rows over, straining to read their Markings.

Doctor. Councilman. Scientist. Coach. Counsellor. Trainer. *I definitely wouldn't want that Marking*, Annona thought, smiling to herself.

"So, without further ado, let's give a warm welcome to Akim, an Elder Harvester in the Land of Rolling Hills."

Annona snapped her head to the stage, her entire being jolting to an abrupt halt.

"What did he just say?" she spoke aloud. The Marked sitting in front of her half turned herself around to face Annona, her lips curled, eyes peering at her. Annona was like a deer in headlights, each one of her senses activated. She stared at the stage, wondering if she had misheard the presenter. Angered that she had not been paying attention, she waited for something to develop.

The presenter took a step back, his arm outstretched as he invited one of the crowd to join him on the stage. Annona stared at the back of the head as it wavered like a buoy in rough waters, chopping through the narrow aisles, past the seated members, and climbed up the steps to the stage. Without doubt, it was Akim. His walk was distinct, even amongst the crowd. He placed his hand out, shaking the hand of the presenter as he turned towards the audience, bearing a warm smile.

Annona dropped down in her seat. Slouching as low as she could, she tucked her head down to the floor so he could not see her. The hall was filled with over four hundred members, the chances of him spotting her were slim. But, Annona wasn't using common sense. All she could feel was panic, like the room had just shrunken into the size of a closet—with one wrong move their eyes might lock, her ambiguity and anonymity blown. Her foot accidentally kicked the chair in front of her, causing it to jolt. The member whipped her head back at Annona, hurling another look of disapproval. Annona did not care this time. She sank further down in the chair.

"Akim, we are so delighted that you came from the Land of Rolling Hills to share with us today," exclaimed the presenter as he placed his hand on Akim's shoulder. "We know that you've been serving there for over twenty-seven rotations around the sun, which is extraordinary."

"By His grace," Akim slipped in.

"Yes, by His grace," the presenter agreed. "Can you tell us what it's been like, to give your life to pursuing your Marking?"

Akim nodded his head then faced the crowd, "First, I want to say thanks for having me here today."

Annona situated herself so she could see him clearly through the spaces between the crowd's heads. He looked more weathered and tired than when she had seen him last, several seasons ago. She noticed he stood with his weight on his good side, still cradling the injury in his knee.

"The Painter Marked me with Harvester, many, many seasons ago," he began. "When I first received my Marking, I resisted it. In fact, I refused to be a Harvester. I thought that from both the Relics I had collected and where my passions were inclined to, that the Painter would have given me the Marking of Designer or Architect, because that was what I loved to do." Akim was slowly pacing from one end of the stage to the other, limping as he crossed the platform. Annona closed her eyes, listening to his voice as it brought her back to the fields, to the breaking of bread in his home.

"So, because I assumed I knew better than the Painter,"—a few around Annona chuckled, glancing at each other with smirks—"I pursued the knowledge required to become a Designer, doing all I could to oppose this Marking that had been stained across my chest." Akim swiped his hands across his Marking, pausing on the left side of the stage.

"My love for the Artist was genuine. I did not pursue becoming a Designer as an act of disobedience, but instead I thought He would see how I knew what was best for me—that I could still bring good to the

Ends of the Earth doing what I preferred." Akim chuckled, shaking his head as he limped to the centre of the stage.

"Although the Artist could use my efforts of being a Designer for good, it never truly satisfied me. I experienced a gnawing in my heart, in my soul, where I felt like something was missing." Akim placed his hand over the centre of his chest, his vision searching the crowd from one end of the hall to the other. Annona dropped even lower into her chair, hoping to melt into the wooden floor.

"I went to the Shepherd of the Gallery I was attending to seek guidance on what could be done to stop the nagging in my heart. The turmoil was keeping me up at night, preventing me from focusing on the projects in front of me. I was even isolating myself from my friends and family." The presenter on stage was nodding his head, his eyes squinting as he looked out amongst the crowd.

"Of course, the Shepherd told me I was unsatisfied because I was not following the Marking across my chest. He challenged me to try it, even for one moon cycle to determine if it would bring any fulfillment to my life. To see if perhaps the Painter did in fact know what He was doing." A second wave of chuckling rippled through the crowd, perceiving how this story would end.

Akim cleared his throat. It did nothing to ease the raspiness from his voice. "As I'm certain you presumably can imagine, the first moon cycle turned into two cycles. With ease it led into a rotation around the sun, which led into a lifetime of harvesting. The fulfillment and purpose I discovered in pursuing my Marking was—and is—the most rewarding accomplishment." Akim paused for effect as a picture appeared on the screen behind him. A beautiful, breathtaking view of the fields with the setting sun dipping over the mountains, creating an angelic flare. His back to the image, he smiled at the crowd as they clapped. Annona immediately identified the land, as it was the place where she had given five seasons of her life, planting and harvesting in those very fields. Tears welled in her eyes, the ache in her heart beat against her chest, a sour lump developed in her throat.

"I can tell you that harvesting has not been easy, especially in a place like the Land of Rolling Hills. The ground is as tough as cement; the resources are limited and outdated; the workers come and go."

With those words a dagger of guilt sunk into her heart, an ache swelled within her chest, while a condescending whisper of shame rippled throughout her body.

"It requires a very dedicated member of the Marked to have what it takes to remain in the Land of Four Seasons. But, what I can attest to is that when you are following your Marking and are obedient to what the Artist has put in front of you, every ounce of pain, suffering, and sacrifice is worth it. Simply spoken, there is nothing else that compares to following your Marking." Akim smiled to the crowd. The image faded from the fields to the faces of children, dressed in rags, but smiling from ear to ear. Collectively, the crowd awed and cooed at the picture.

A saddened joy illuminated from their eyes. Annona felt the ache press in harder, finding a path into her soul. The ache stormed against the doors of her heart, against the barriers she built to keep the dam from flooding and washing her away. Annona gazed back at the saddened joy through her watery vision. The guilt crashed against her, like waves in a cove. *I've forgotten their faces. How have I forgotten their faces? How could I have left them?* These weren't pictures of strangers; Annona knew each child by name. She knew their favourite colours, their favourite foods, the names of their family and friends. The photos dismantled the dam she had established in her heart to keep the feelings of longing and ache at bay. The pain flooded into every muscle and bone in her body.

"Wow, Akim, thanks for sharing your story with us," the presenter said, resting his hand on Akim's back. "Akim will be in the atrium after today's talk, so if you're interested in getting involved with harvesting or planting in the Land of Rolling Hills, or learning more about his story, don't hesitate to stop by." The crowd cheered and applauded as Akim gave a modest wave, hobbling his way off the stage and returning to his seat.

There was no way Annona would be able to sit through the rest of the talk. She was undone, like an avalanche plummeting at a hundred miles an hour, like a sandstorm churning in the midst of the desert. She was consumed by guilt, anger, and fury. Annona raised herself to her feet, preparing for a quick exit. She slouched low as she walked through the row and quietly pushed through the exit doors. The presenter continued talking, but his voice was muffled compared to Annona's inner voice, which screamed *get out, get out, get out!*

She rushed as quickly as she could for the doors to leave the Gallery, dripping with tears as anxiety and guilt overwhelmed her. Pulling on her shirt, she frantically covered her Marking, terrified someone from the Gallery would ask her if she wanted to speak with Akim.

How embarrassed she would be, to see him, when who she was now was not a fraction of who she had been when living in her Marking. Moon cycles had passed, and she had nothing to show— nothing she had done helped to progress her Masterpiece. She couldn't even recall the last time she looked at it.

Akim's last words to her in the Land of Rolling Hills, "Do good," were supposed to encourage her to carry on in her Marking. Instead the words had done nothing but wreaked havoc inside her mind, like a hornet thrown into a jar and rattled. His words had done little to inspire her. In fact, they haunted her, ravaging her thoughts until she would drown out the words with the help of Persipaó.

Frantically, she located the exit doors as she rounded the corner. It felt as if the oxygen had been sucked out of the Gallery. The doors burst open as she threw her entire weight into them. Annona sucked back air as she raced down the stairs to the cobblestone road, her foot missing the last step. She tumbled forward, stumbling a few feet ahead before she caught her balance.

She heard the crunch of the gravel. Annona halted, keeping her eyes on her sneakers. Her breathing was rampant, panting from her fall but also the ache swarming in her soul.

"This was a mistake, this was *such* a mistake," Annona said. "Why would I think I could find comfort there? This was all a huge mistake!"

"You made the mistake, Annona, when you abandoned your Marking," Kachash said as it emerged from the shadows of the Alley, sliding toward her. "You dumped your Marking and escaped as soon as it got too demanding. *You* abandoned those who were suffering. You truly are nothing but a failure."

Annona tried to take in a large breath of air, but her breath felt sharp against her lungs. *I want to go home, but this isn't my home. I have no home.*

Angō had attached itself to Annona sometime between her exit and her stumble. It was with her so often that Annona could no longer sense its coming and goings.

Tears streamed down her cheeks as she wiped them away. The thought of crossing through the Alley to find refuge in the comfort of her home sent her mind into a fleeting panic. To see the crowd suffering, when all she could think about was her own pain riddled her with guilt.

"Come now, Annona," said Perispaó. It flicked dust from its shoes as it came from behind Kachash. It placed a hand on Annona's shoulder, giving a tight squeeze. Its pointed chin seemed more crooked than it had appeared before. The sight of it gave Annona the creeps, but its offer of comfort was too easy to resist. "You've had a horrible day. Let's go home and relax. I can help you find things to do to take your mind away from all of this."

Annona nodded her head slowly. Perispaó offered its arm, and Annona hooked hers around willingly. Guiding her, they traveled the route most often taken by avoiding the Alley. Together they walked the extra three blocks to her home, not once did she turn back.

25

ACHING

Take two sticks and rub them together. At first, nothing notable will arise. The outer layers of bark will knead against one another and scrape off each other's skins. Continue grinding them with the same amount of pressure, and the inner layers of the sticks will make contact, generating friction between the two. If the intensity of the stress is increased, the friction will lead to heat. It may be strenuous, but as the sticks continue to grind together, the heat will intensify, resulting in combustion. When the flicker of a spark has started, blow oxygen, slowly, steadily. The spark will turn itself into a flame, and with that flame, you initiate fire. The flame can destroy homes, blaze villages into ashes, and turn fields to dust.

Fire unleashed in Annona. Relentless rubbing of anger and ache—the two sticks of pain. Restraining her emotions acted as a breath to the flame. Sparks flew out of control which landed in her belly, and the oxygen caused the fire. The fire in her belly unleashed to the organs in her body, resulting in the expulsion of the sorrow in her heart, the rancid thoughts in her mind, and the anger that now reached to the tips of her fingers.

She ached, oh how her heart ached! When the anger subsided, undesirable emotions flooded in. Aching. Longing. Desire. Wishing. Wanting. Annona mourned for the life she had lost, the ache consuming the hole her purpose once occupied. It was all she sensed, formed out of the absence of the Land of Rolling Hills. Her heart ached for a purpose, for passion, and for joy.

Anger and aching, hand in hand, guided her steps throughout her day. It felt as if her anger was tethered to electricity. She sought to contain her thoughts like she did in the beginning, when she had first arrived back to the Land of Four Seasons, but it was no use. The ache festered into a wound in her heart, her heart supplying the ache to the rest of her body.

It would seep out now and then, the anger and the ache, in the moments she least expected. Someone would converse about farming and her mind would relate it to harvesting, and within seconds the uncontrollable tears would shed. A tune would play in the Gallery that used to be her battle cry. Now, she would grind her teeth, white knuckling the back of the chair in front of her. Her mouth closed, refusing to sing the words, her mind recalling ten million reflections of her failures. She found herself frantic for the song to be over.

Her own mind terrified her. It was like carrying a beast inside, a beast eating her from the inside out. Would it consume her if she were to allow it? If she were to truly realize what she had abandoned and what she had given up, she knew that the sadness would swallow her whole.

Annona realized she had no control. Her mind refused to be restrained from the ruminating cries of her deepest fears. She possessed no control of the crowd who would continue to ask her questions about the Land of Rolling Hills, desiring more than the superficial answer she had to offer. She could not escape the tunes that would play, in markets, stores, or the Gallery. How could she stop herself from seeing items that would remind her of the harvest? Buying a replacement watch did nothing to interrupt her from remembering the harvest. The purchase was nothing more than a feeble attempt to distract herself with something temporal and tangible. Everything she hid from Desert's Stone under her bed or in the back of her closet were landmines. Being anywhere within their proximity, even though hidden, still set off her anger and heart's ache. She had no control over the savage anger that would reveal its teeth to her loved ones, snapping its jaws at whomever it chose. Everything was out of her control; her sole option was to pick up the mangled pieces she would leave in the aftermath of her uncensored reaction.

The shame Annona experienced was like nothing she had ever faced before. The shame overtook the foundational beliefs in Annona's life. She no longer believed she was a child of the Artist, nor that she deserved His grace, nor that she was loved. She concluded she was a failure. This new foundation was set with so many fractures and jagged edges that self-anger and hatred oozed from her heart.

Annona herself was damaged goods attempting to control the victims of her peripheral wake. A shell of who she once was, her only responsibility at that moment was to attempt to retain still waters amidst choppy seas. Impossible, yet she tried. Tried to preserve the remaining relationships she had intact, tried to not upset herself with thoughts of the harvest, and tried to replay the events that had led up to her leaving and what she had done wrong. Her mind desperately tried to sort out what had happened, but her attempts were as feeble as attempts trying to flatten a wave. Her ache would drown her, like a feather tied to a chain and anchor, unloaded into the bottomless ocean. Sinking, sinking, sinking.

She understood where she needed to go, but she dreaded the thought of going there. Annona tried to go earlier, when she had first returned to the Land of Four Seasons, but she couldn't muster the energy in her bones. The desperation was not deep enough to motivate her feet to want to move. But not anymore. The pain was so staggering it was like she was gasping for oxygen, perpetually in the state of taking half breaths, incapable of filling her lungs with the air she was so desperate for. She was living a half-life. The anger and ache consumed more and more of her life. It had no sense of boundaries. No other options were available to her. She would have to make the journey even though her entire being resisted it. She was sick of the free fall into darkness, the impact of hitting the ground below couldn't be as volatile as the constant barrelling out of control.

In the beginning she believed the instincts of anger and aching would run their course and eventually burn out, but the fires of anger and ache always found new pieces within her to sustain its slow, toxic burn.

Unintentionally, Annona fueled the fires within her. Distractions through projects and work did nothing to extinguish its flames. Isolating herself from the crowd resulted in her own voice repeating in her head. Attempts to control her thoughts and environments revealed that she possessed no control. Her strategies enhanced the flames, strengthened the fire, and intensified the heat. Her efforts were not working.

The complication was that Annona could no longer continue, not with the fires of anger and ache roaring inside her. The pain hurt too much—it demanded a resolution, whatever it may be. The time for something to die drew near.

Her dream was already dead.

Life held no purpose.

Everything, from this point forward, was meaningless.

The symptoms. I have the symptoms. I am asking the questions. I am Markless.

She put on her shoes, slipped into her jacket, shoved her hands in her pockets, and headed to the bowels of her pain, bracing herself to face the darkness head on at the Altar.

Part V

The True Marking

I saw a great many bones on the floor of the valley, bones that were very dry. 'Dry bones, hear the word of the Lord! This is what the Sovereign Lord says to these bones: I will make breath enter you, and you will come to life. I will attach tendons to you and make flesh come upon you and cover you with skin; I will put breath in you, and you will come to life. Then you will know that I am the Lord.'

Ezekiel 37—Paraphrased

26

POWERS OF DARKNESS

As Annona approached the border of the Altar, she slowed her pace. She had considered turning around dozens of times, and as the border approached, the feeling only intensified. She stared into the grey sky that peaked through the wooden giants; beyond them lay her sacred place. She turned back to the way she had come, feeling foolish for expecting—perhaps demanding—a confrontation. Proceeding to the Altar would mean arriving at the end of an era and a resolution to the pain. But, she couldn't go back. Something had to end.

"This might have been a mistake," she mumbled to herself. "I'm not ready to face this." Annona was numb to Angō's presence, its cables and wires embedded in her cycle's ago, making it difficult to differentiate which voice was hers and which voice was not. She had become accustomed to clouded vision and did not care nor think to ask the Painter to distinguish its voice from hers.

Maybe it was an outer force, or just a still, small voice pleading with her to press forward, either way her legs propelled her toward the Altar.

She reached the perimeter of the field where the wooden giants surrounded the patch. She glanced down at her feet, and considered taking off her shoes, but as a quiet act of defiance decided against it. Everything had been so ambiguous, she doubted that the Painter would speak with her. She wasn't sure anything good would come out of visiting the Altar, but she had exhausted all other options. Life, or whichever word used to determine a half-lived life, wasn't worth living anymore.

Annona groaned, stepping beyond the border of the field, gazing upon the tops of the leaves, scanning the view of the wooden giants. Nothing had changed over the past six rotations around the sun. It was the same, but aged. The grass grew thicker and the flowers had multiplied. As far as Annona could tell, the Altar had remained untouched. She walked to the heart of the field, her feet moving heavily and her breathing accelerated as she stood silently looking out into the clouded grey sky. The dew on the grass was thick, as the morning sun had not yet risen. Was the sun still in existence, merely hidden under layers of slated clouds? Or had it disappeared just like the purpose of her hands, her heart, and her mind—gone as soon as it had come?

As her tearful vision extended across the tops of the wooden giants, the silence ate at her, inducing her limbs to twitch. She heard the hum in her ears, the beat of her pumping heart, the saliva clicking as it stuck to the roof of her mouth, and her lungs filling and discharging the air. The ringing in her ears became more concentrated, sounding like an alarm. She inhaled air, and calmly released it through her lips, trying to settle her nerves.

Breathe in and out. She sensed the anger and ache swarming inside, refusing to be calmed. Her normal rhythm of breathing, calm and subdued, was heightening, intensifying, and quickening. Her heart and lungs felt as if they were being controlled by her emotions, not listening to her mind as it told her to slow down. Her breathing turned into panting, providing oxygen for the fire to breed, growing violent inside her, until she could hold it in no longer and it had to be expelled from her.

Annona cried out, not with her lungs, but with every pore, organ, and cell inside her body. The energy of anger swarmed like hornets to every muscle and every vein within her, causing her body to crumple and tighten as she released the anger and ache out of her gaping mouth. She freed the fury, forcing it out of her lungs for as long as she could. Her spit flew, her voice was cracked and raw. She collapsed to the ground once the last segment of sound uttered out from her lips, her mouth drooling, hands grasping lumps of grass and dirt. She panted, the anger still brooding her mind, the hornets of anger stinging her body.

Not enough, it wasn't enough. Her knees buckled as she pushed herself back up to her feet. She stumbled a few steps forward. She wiped the spit from her face with the back of her hand. *Deeper, dig deeper.*

She burrowed further into her lungs, sucked back air, and screamed again—this time louder, finding more power in her body.

A memory flashed before her eyes of when she was a child, left alone in a historic Gallery. She had found an organ staged in the front of the sanctuary. She climbed up onto the bench and pressed on a single key. The sound bellowed around her, like a train passing on the tracks. The pipes of the organ had been mounted on each wall of the sanctuary, making the sound ubiquitous. An idea raised in her mind to hold as many keys as possible to produce a horrific sound. She used her arms, hands, and feet, extending her fingers as wide as they could. All at once she pressed them: the pedals on the floor, the two rows of keys. The sound was deafening, sour, all-consuming. The notes boomed through her little body, shaking her. The vibrations reverberated within her heart. The sound terrified her. Now, from within her, the same sour chord or anger and ache spilled out from her lips, the sound unleashed from deep within her lungs, escaping into the dawn, across the Altar.

Ugly, cracked, and coarse, the sound ripped out of her. A torrent of painful memories she had been protecting herself from flashed before her eyes: the Marking ceremony, anticipating her leave, packing of her things, arriving to the Land of Rolling Hills, starting the harvest, the thousands of hours of work in the fields, the suffering crowds, her mistakes with the weeds, the abandoning workers, Jore abandoning his

Mark, the overwhelming work, the burnout, the disappointment in the Elder's eyes, her waste of time at her current position, her forsaking of her own Marking, and, finally, the perpetual presence of anger and ache. What she could never before put to words, the ache and anger, was finally able to be released.

She felt her throat shredding as she carried the last of the sound, the taste of copper filling her mouth. Screaming her pain still wasn't enough. The questions she had permitted to invade her soul, which produced cracks into her foundation, now raised up from within her. She was no longer standing on solid ground.

"Where were You! Why have You abandoned me? Why did You leave me? What was that? What *was* this disaster, this utter failure, that *You* put me through? Why me, *why*? Everything I did, I did it for You!" Annona fell to her knees, harsh sobs rushing out of her. The urge to vomit arose. She knelt, on her knees, head bowed. She remained that way for some time, releasing the anger and the ache in defeat. She didn't know when the screaming had evolved into crying until she heard her own whimpering and sobs.

"Remove this Marking from me," Annona said, her eyes remaining closed.

Suddenly, Annona heard a rustle coming from the bushes at the bottom of the incline. She slowly raised her eyes to discover the shadows of six figures weaving themselves past the wooden giants, tiptoeing into the clearing. One of them levitated several feet off the ground, hovering over their bodies. Her eyes squinted, trying to recognize the shadows that were trudging towards her.

Powers of Darkness entering the Altar

Shuffling closer, they produced no sound, but continued to crawl, slither, and stride toward her. Only a few feet away, she still struggled to view their faces. The dawn's light had not yet broke, casting shadows over their faces. When they were within an arm's length she finally recognized them: Kachash, Perispaó, the Brothers, Mirmah, and Yirah.

Yirah had not yet exposed itself to Annona, although she sensed its characteristics throughout her whole life. She was told stories of Yirah when she was a child—always accounts of warning. She knew few of the crowd who had been consumed by Yirah, leaving them incapable of pursuing their Marking. Yirah did not reveal itself often, only in the most opportune moments, when it found its victims weak and unfit to resist.

Annona imagined what Yirah looked like when she was told stories, but it proved more terrifying than her imagination could have conjured. Yirah, by far, was the most frightening of them all. It did not possess a shape like that of the crowd, nor the form of a wild beast. It looked like a black sheet: a surface of silk, being tossed and thrashed in the air. Annona had seen moonless nights and explored sunless caves, but this shade of black was strikingly dark—it was like nothing she had ever encountered before. The ebony sheet swirled all around, out of control like smoke, as if a force of wind were blowing beneath it, keeping it suspended from the ground. Annona was unsure whether it had control or was being forced by the winds—it would rise up suddenly then snap back towards the ground: swirling, rotating, twisting, and strangling.

Fear. Unleashed and un-adulturated. She felt a rush of blood to the head. The putrid, copper taste in her throat could not be swallowed as her mouth was dry. She forced herself to swallow. Pain shot through her throat from her damaged vocal cords. Her mind and instincts felt primal as dread overtook her. Utterly helpless, she didn't know what to do. She was frozen in her panic, dumbfounded by fear.

Confidently, they crept closer to her, eyes trained on Annona, not withdrawing their stare for even a second. Each step shifted forward in precise unison, their bodies swayed rhythmically with one another—orchestrated by a master conductor. Yirah snapped and cracked over their heads. Annona was still on her knees as they approached her within striking distance.

"You have failed, your dream is dead," Kachash said. The tar spat from its mouth and splattered the top of Annona's head, trickling down her face.

For the first time, Perispaó's voice was not the soothing voice that normally spoke to Annona, but screeched like a hog making its course to the slaughter, the sound piercing her ears. "Nothing you produce will ever relieve the pain. No distraction will numb the hurt of your wound. You will always sense that brokenness within you."

Annona wept silently, paralyzed with fear, afraid that if she made too much movement they would strike. She kept her head down as she slowly tucked her knees together and pulled her arms in close, doing anything she could to make herself smaller.

"Everything happens for a reason, but you will learn no lesson out of this. Your suffering was unnecessary, an act of cruelty!" the Brothers chanted in unison with one another, laughing as they tumbled and climbed on top of each other.

"Meaningless, meaningless, everything you did in the Land of Rolling Hills was meaningless. Everything you will do is worthless!" Angō said.

Angō's cables and wires twisted and contracted into each other, the loose ends made contact which caused sparks to fly, landing on the ground beside Annona. Small fires combusted on the small blades of grass. Annona saw the fires out of the corner of her eyes, spreading quickly to the meadow around her. She could feel the heat, but she was still too afraid to move.

Mirmah ducked down, its eyes at the same level of Annona. It silently waited until Annona hesitantly lifted her head. Its ornaments and awards glistened from the glow of the surrounding flames. Her body trembled. Mirmah tilted its head and softly said, "I wasn't able to get you to leave at first, but low and behold, you left on your own!" it laughed, "The Painter gave you a Marking knowing you would fail in and demonstrate your worthlessness." As soon as it uttered the message it grinned, amused with itself, withdrawing back in position with the others.

Annona felt a surge of air blow over her head, hearing Yirah directly above her, like the alarming sound of the wings of a hornet. Swirling above her head, it snapped above her hair. A sound erupted: a high-pitched squeal. Annona looked at Perispaó, but it wasn't responsible for the sound. The sound heightened all around her. She slowly looked up, to the being above her head, only to find the source of the sickening squeal as belonging to Yirah. Its voice sounded like a vacuum sucking in glass and metal, while a lost scream of agony reverberated from somewhere within Yirah's body. The two sounds competed for volume. It was piercing, disturbing, and haunting.

"They've abandoned you, just as you've abandoned your Marking. You're useless, you have no purpose," Yirah said, its voice scratchy and squealing. Annona lowered her head and focused her eyes back on the dirt beneath her.

Over and over and over again they recited these lines as Annona knelt, weeping desperately. Their statements were no longer heard outside of her head but now embedded within her mind. The tone of her own voice repeated their mantras like a twisted lullaby. The surrounding air became ice cold, intensifying to the force of a hurricane, the sky blackening.

In a trance, they swayed in unison toward Annona, chanting their messages of destruction. Annona was too terrified to lift her eyes to their distorted faces, keeping her head to the ground. If she dared to looked up, she would have found herself face-to-face with her deepest fears.

In that moment, as they taunted her, it was as if she had forgotten everything that she had once known to be true. She possessed the power to silence them. She—*with one word!*—could end her suffering. But, she had forgotten her foundational truths. For too many seasons she allowed her foundation to be saturated with cracks of doubt, fear, and anger. Lies she told herself became her new half-truths. She had silenced the voice within her that spoke contrary, so the lies presented as truth. The Darkness knew this. They pressed in with their ploys, to tear her down and consume her while she was forgetting.

"You are a failure, unable and incapable of doing any good for the crowd." Kachash's black tar had left spots all over Annona, from the top of her head to the tips of her toes.

"The pain you feel is eternal, and nothing will distract you from your gaping wound," Persipaó said, rubbing her arms, shoulders, legs—whatever it could touch to massage the lies into her.

"All of your hardships and trials you went through were meaningless. Look how your pain has established such a weak character in you, rendering you useless," the Brothers bellowed in unison, climbing on top of her, jumping on her shoulders then tumbling off.

"Meaningless. Your life is meaningless!" Angō chanted, its electricity heightened. It flashed bolts like lightening and created a firestorm around her. Annona could no longer see the wooden giants through the flames and smoke. Its sparks, fuelled by Kachash's tar, had caught fire to the grass. The flames circled around her, Annona in the centre of the ring.

"Your failures have caused others of the Marked to burnout, not just you. You deserted the fields in the time of their greatest need," Mirmah spat, its face grotesque.

"You, Annona, have been abandoned by the Artist. You are useless. You have no purpose. Your life of value is over," Yirah whispered, levitating all around her, kicking up the dirt and dust from the ground. "If your life of worth is over, what is the point of living?" The dust caught fire in the electrical cloud as Annona sat helpless in the eye of the storm.

It is over for me. I have failed. My dream is dead. I will never find happiness.

He has abandoned me. I am worthless, I have no purpose, Annona recited in her mind.

Kachash, Persipaó, Angō, Mirmah, the Brothers, and Yirah all reached out toward her and placed their skeletal fingers inches above Annona's Marking. Angō's shockwaves pulsed with a vengeance. In perfect unison, the tones of their voice reverberated together as one, "We can stop your misery, just ask, and we will carry out what the Artist will not." Their reach steadily lowered towards her chest, the fabric of her shirt about to make contact with the palms of their clutch.

At that moment a crack—powerful, like thunder—caused her ears to pop and the chanting to abruptly cease. The ground she knelt on shook and rumbled followed by the sound of water sizzling on a hot pan, paper shredding into scraps, and chains being bound and shackled.

Annona remained on her knees, head down, too frightened to look up.

Am I dead?

27

LIGHT SHINES THROUGH DARKNESS

The stifling air that surrounded her became cool, and the wind hushed to a gentle breeze. She couldn't be dead, her lungs were filling with oxygen.

"Annona, Annona."

It was Him. It was His voice; His calm, and precious voice. The voice that could soothe any weeping heart, the voice that spoke with authority over the dark principalities, the voice she had sworn to herself she would never forget... *but the one that she had.* The voice settled beside her, whispering in her ear. It was the Artist's voice. He crouched down beside her. His arm on Annona's shoulders, He lifted her chin. Annona opened her eyes. He was staring at her, His eyes rimmed with tears. He gave Annona a moment to see that she was safe.

The Artist had come for her. The Artist had stilled the storm.

The Artist had bound the dark principalities in chains, their mouths covered with cloth, their eyes sealed with scales. Chains wrapped around their bodies, fastening them to the earth, binding them to the dust. The Artist looked at Annona, then concentrated on the principalities. Without looking at her, the Artist whispered, "Cast them from your sight."

With all the courage she could muster in her throat, she yelled, "In the Name of the Artist, return to the pits of the earth! Rid yourselves from me!"

Before Annona spoke the final word, the tormenters exploded into a cloud of smog, scattering the dust and grass around them. Not a second passed before the smog was sucked into the earth like funnels—not one of them surviving.

The Artist turned to Annona. Wasting no time, His hands wiped off Kachash's tar from her legs and arms. Everywhere He touched it appeared as if He had washed clean. This gesture of goodness completely undid her. She dropped her head to her knees and wept.

Annona, embarrassed, raised her eyes to His. His face wet with tears, His eyes washed over her with concern and care. When He finished cleaning off the tar, He stared into her eyes. Tears streamed down His face. Seeing the Artist demonstrating real emotion from her pain, Annona's heart swelled with sadness. She dropped her eyes as He studied her for a moment; speaking no words as they wept. Rays of light peaked through the horizon, rushing past the darkened clouds.

Angō's fires had been extinguished. Debris left from the chaos of Yirah was scattered around the meadow. She remained in the centre, Annona with the Artist in the aftermath of the storm.

He helped to lift her from her knees to her feet, and as she stood He wiped the tears from her cheeks, moving her hair to the side of her face. Annona's eyes traced over where the dark principalities had been bound, feeling too much shame to look at Him.

Annona swallowed and winced from the rawness in her throat, inflamed from the violent screaming. The Artist took His hands and placed them on either side of her neck, positioning His thumbs on the centre of her throat. Pushing slightly with His thumbs, the pressure numbed the pain as the taste of sweet honey spread on her tongue. She swallowed, the liquid soothed the shreds in her vocal cords, overpowering the taste of copper. The pain in her throat vanished. He released His hands. Annona half smiled at Him, raising her eyes to His.

The Artist resembled the Painter: a similar form of body, style of hair, and colour of eyes. It was Him, but it was not Him. Slight differences were apparent in His posture, the shape of His nose, the structure of His jaw, and in the manner in which He held Himself. She looked deeper into His eyes. The colour on first glance had appeared the same, but Annona began noticing speckles of grey and blue near His iris. In His mannerisms and in all these slight differences it was still Him—the same, but different. He was dressed similar to the Painter, but the apron He wore was black. The contrast of the paint stood out from His apron, the splatters reminded her of her Marking Ceremony with the Painter. But there was residue of other material on His apron as well. Annona noticed clay and dust, the materials of a Potter. In the front pocket was a few small chisels, rasps, and hammers; the tools of a Sculptor.

"I know the ugly is there, Annona. No need to hide what I already see," the Artist said as the corners of His mouth slightly raised and His eyes squinted. He placed His hand inside one of His pockets while the other settled on her shoulder.

Annona shook her head and swallowed. It was now, the moment she had been waiting for, the chance for her to face the accusations, lay the charges, and discharge her pain. To release the ache that had been eroding in her heart, concealed deep within the bowels of anguish. This conversation wasn't going to take place with the Shepherd or through the mouths of the Marked, she was going head to head with the Artist—He made Himself real to her, so she would release everything to Him.

"You left me, Artist. *You* deserted *me*. All I ever wanted to do was to serve You, to go wherever You called me, to pursue my Marking with an intense passion for You." Her eyes sank to the ground, her hands falling to her side. She continued, cautioning herself to stay calm. She felt her hands trembling beside her. The Artist slid His hand down her arm, squeezing her hand. He held it until the trembling stopped. She returned to His face. As the Artist took a deep breath in and out, Annona synched her breathing to His.

"Tell me more," the Artist prompted.

Annona bit her lower lip, and continued, "You were the One who showed me those Relics, who inspired me to choose what I did. You are the One who created me, who knit me together in my mother's womb, who knows when I lay down and when I rise. You are the One who gives gifts, talents, and passions. Did You not instill an ache within me to help those in need, the anguish invading the depths of my heart? The Painter—*You*—placed a Marking on me and presented me with the chance to harvest. You saw what that meant, that I would give all I am to it, and I did. I sacrificed, I suffered, and I pushed myself hard." The truth animated Annona, she was no longer calm. She had released herself from His embrace, her hands flying, voice cracking, and unable to stand still.

"I missed events, I missed family, I missed relationships of those who passed, I missed funerals, for what? For it to collapse on itself, to implode in on itself, to fall apart into a million shattered pieces? This was not a momentary decision for me, Artist. I gave my best to learn what it was the crowd endured when I lived in the Land of Rolling Hills. I advocated for those whose voices were being suppressed. I stood for those who needed a hand. I tried to be conscientious of what I aligned myself with, and if it took advantage of the oppressed, I wouldn't have anything to do with it." Annona's memories stung her tongue as they escaped her mouth, but she wasn't finished.

"When the Planters and Harvesters abandoned their Marking, what did I do? Did I pack it in? No, I worked twice as hard, picking up what they left behind. I tried my best. How was I supposed to control them from abandoning their Markings?"

The Artist remained quiet, listening intently. He kept His eyes locked on hers, nodding His head, giving Annona the encouragement to continue.

"I became burned out because You wouldn't send any workers. I grew weary because the harvest was plentiful and there were not enough Harvesters. Isn't the crowd Yours? Aren't *You* the one who should care for them? I was trying to help them, but it no longer was a selfless act. Instead, it wore me down, destroying my spirit. The need was too great. I couldn't give it all." Annona was speaking so quickly that she stumbled on her words, choking on them as they spilled from her lips.

"I was forced to return because of my burnout and exhaustion, because I couldn't keep up with the harvest. Do you understand how much that hurt? To know there is a harvest, a plentiful one, and that I cannot be part of it? That there is good work to be done, but I am here, undertaking tasks that possess no significance, have no contribution to my Masterpiece, that have nothing to do with what my hands, my heart, and my mind can give itself naturally to?"

Annona shook her head, figuring she had disclosed too much by now. At this point she knew if there was a line that shouldn't have been crossed, she had sailed passed it a moment ago. Yet, He didn't say anything to stop her. His silence angered her.

"Why would You give me the Marking of Harvester only for it to be my greatest failure—to be stripped away from me? The Marking of Harvester, the failed calling of who I was to be, remains across my chest. Its sole purpose is to remind me each and every day I am a failure. I want the Marking removed, and I want it erased from my chest! It's a lie. I am not a Harvester, I am a fraud!" She tore herself away from Him, grasping on to the neck of her shirt as she ripped it halfway down, exposing the Marking of Harvester across her chest. "You want the Marking to remind me each day of how I failed You? Of how I wasn't *enough* for You, not *worthy* enough for the harvest and remaining in pursuit of my Marking?" She beat wildly against her Marking, "Not *good* enough, not *strong* enough, not *brave* enough... incapable of enduring hardships, pathetic enough to burnout after five seasons?" Annona caught her breath, panting while her body shook with anger, the ache seeping from her bones.

"It aches, Artist, it aches so badly. I don't recognize who I am. I don't see what my purpose is any longer. I want what I can't have. I am so lost. Where is my home? Who am I? *Oh, it aches*!" Annona cried, heaving so hard that her entire body crumbled.

The Artist kept His watch on Annona. He refrained from defending Himself. He did not use words to comfort her. He stood quiet, allowing Annona to surrender what had been accumulating in her for so long.

She used her hands to cover her face. Heavy sobs of anger heaved from within her, the ache spilling out like water. He remained silent. Time slowly crept on as her sobs became tears and eventually diminished to a small trickle, watering the dry earth below.

28

TRUTH & GRACE

"My sweet, sweet Annona," the Artist whispered, stepping closer to her. "My beautiful, loving Annona." He reached His hands to her clenched grip, taking her hands away from covering her face. He placed her hands inside His, His fingers wrapping around her grasp, His right hand covering both of hers. Annona pulled her hand away as she wiped a stray tear from her cheek, the Artist blinked heavily as droplets fell from His eyes.

He sniffed, inhaling air before He spoke, His words saturated in gentleness. "I know the Marking the Painter gave you—*that We gave you*—and I delight in the talents and the gifts you have, because I inspired them, like a breath of air to a flame. I am proud of what your hands, your heart, and your mind give itself naturally to, without selfish ambition, because I am the one who formed the prints of your hands, who gave blood to your pumping heart, and who established the dreams and hopes that would light up your mind." He smiled as He pointed at her heart, then lightly touched the side of her head, tucking a loose strain of hair behind her ear. The Artist sifted the hairs between His thumb and forefinger, His eyes welled with tears as He held back a sob. He slid His hands back to hers.

"The beauty of the Land of Rolling Hills brought you delight. You loved the mountains, found charm in the sunsets, and the night skies that shined uncountable stars reminded you of my goodness. I, the Sculptor, the Potter, and the Painter, was the One who appointed the perfect placement of each spectacle, deliberately placing each wooden giant, each hill, and each star. I did not do this in vain. We created every piece of creation with you in mind, knowing how it would bring you closer to Us, which is Our deepest heart's desire." The Artist's eyes skimmed across the tops of the wooden giants, smiling as He looked upon the pure beauty of the towers, something Annona had done thousands of times before.

"But it wasn't the beauty of the land that kept me there, Artist. There is beauty here in the Land of Four Seasons, some landscapes unmatchable to the Ends of the Earth. There was a bond I had in the Land of Rolling Hills that was much greater than my admiration for the scenery," Annona said.

"The bond is because of your Marking," the Artist said.

"Of course it is! It has *everything* to do with my Marking." Annona shouted, her hands thrown to the air. "On the fields of Desert's Stone, I achieved some of my greatest accomplishments."

"You gave your best effort each day, leaving everything you had on the fields. I saw that," the Artist said, in agreement.

The ache moved in Annona, whispering to her to speak to Him of the cause of so much pain. "It's not just about the fields, it's that I released my heart to the crowd. I would have done anything to end their suffering, and to lessen their pain. I did whatever I could to show I was loyal and willing to sacrifice to helping the crowd find their voice." A tear slipped pass her cheek, her mind's eye remembering the children from the village of Desert's Stone. "I've failed them, I've let them down. It's so overwhelming, to know there is so much brokenness in the Ends of the Earth, and I am doing nothing to help stop it."

His head dipped as He sighed heavily, His hands combed through His hair as He looked at Annona. "Since you have come back to the Land of Four Seasons, you could not find your way out of the unbearable feelings of failure. I have felt your anger, I feel your aches, and I've been more than aware of your suffering."

The Artist rested His arm on Annona, observing her while she took a breath in, validating her pain.

"My sweet, sweet, Annona. I must show you something, something you have overlooked and missed for many seasons." The Artist released her shoulder, His hand dropping to His side.

His statement immediately upset her. Had she missed a Relic she should have collected from her journeying, or did she not realize a gifting that was dormant in her? She felt restless, shifting her feet. She wasn't sure how this could help her now.

The Artist, standing in front of Annona, stepped aside to the right of her. He knelt down, and touched the ground, placing the palm of His hand on the grass. As He raised His hand, the dust lifted from the ground. It formed an outline. As He lifted His hand, it grew. It had feet, then legs, hands, arms, a torso, a chest, neck, and head. From the dust it took form, shifting and moving, but stayed constricted within the outline. The Artist lifted His hand, raising the form, until it stood at the exact same height as Annona. Softly, He released His hand from the top of its head. The form had no breath, it was without definition, and clothed in a simple garment.

The Artist positioned Himself directly in front of the form. Annona could see the side of the Artist's face. He took in a deep breath, His characteristics reminding Annona of the Painter before He transformed Himself into the storm. The Artist blew His breath softly over the form's face, starting from its forehead and ending at its chin.

Annona blinked, and in the split second that her eyes were closed, the form was absolutely defined. She shook her head, unable to comprehend what she saw.

It was her.

Hair for hair, freckle for freckle, pound for pound, Mark for Mark: the Form standing in front of her was Annona.

Annona looked her up and down. The Form in front of her held a modest smile, her hands set to her sides. Annona stepped closer; it was like finding her reflection in a mirror, yet it was like nothing she had experienced before. This was not merely a reflection of herself. It was *her*—identical in flesh. It was as if she had fallen through the reflection of a mirror: no longer constrained by the glass, but swallowed into a new dimension.

The Artist stood still, allowing Annona to observe the Form, giving her mind a chance to capture what her eyes were seeing. The Form was silent, simply breathing: in and out, inhaling and exhaling.

Across the Form's chest was the same Marking of Harvester, identical to her own. Annona lifted her hand, lightly tracing her fingers across her own Marking, touching the bumps and texture of the letters.

The Artist, standing beside the Form, wrapped one arm around her, so they were standing side by side. The Form kept her eyes locked on Annona, Annona returning the stare.

He planted His free hand over the centre of the Form's chest, over the Form's Marking, where her heart lay beneath. He smiled at the Form, then turned His head to Annona. The Artist searched her eyes as an expression of sincerity washed over His face. He tightened His jaw, hair floating gently in the wind.

"Annona, you have been given the Marking of Harvester from the Painter, but you've missed the Mark."

The Artist's eyes returned to the Form, His face somber as He searched the Form's eyes for an answer. A look of confidence glowed within her face; she nodded at Him. The Artist nodded in return, carefully pressing His fingers into the Form's skin. Like fingers sinking into a ball of dough, her skin absorbed His fingers gracefully, but did not tear. With four fingers, He drew the flesh to the side. Annona winced, assuming the Form would cry out. But, the Form's expression of trust remained on her face. No blood dripped as it would with an open wound, her face indicating no pain. He continued to pull the skin back, like pulling aside a curtain to release the light. The letters from the word Harvester pushed into each other, each letter crashing into the one before, wrinkling like a sandbar found on the shore of the ocean. When His fingers and the skin reached her other collar bone He paused, exposing her beating heart. The Artist removed His fingers; the flesh He had pulled back remained still.

A gasp of wonder escaped from Annona's lips as she observed the majestic muscle pump life to the body. Mesmerized, it filled and released, expanded and collapsed, without missing a beat. She jerked her head to the Artist, expecting Him to add context as to why He would show this—her heart—to her. It was then that she noticed out of the corner of her eye something foreign lay across the glassy surface of the beating muscle. It looked like an insignificant scratch, something perhaps scarred over the heart. She stepped closer, straining to see the scratch more clearly. As Annona lowered her head to the form's chest, she could see that it was not a scratch, but a letter. It had only been a portion of the word that had first caught her eye, for as she looked closer the letters were covering the entire surface of the heart.

Across the heart, simply, beautifully, pumping, and worn, was the word "*Mine*."

Across her heart, "Mine."

29

THE ARTIST

Everything, my child, has led to this moment: this sacred revelation of pure wonder and ecstasy. My truth, arise from darkness and do a new thing in my beloved's heart!

Drink it in, Annona. Let the truth heal. Allow it to seep past your gates of iron, and cut through your broken walls.

Ah, my Signature, securing and distinguishing my most beautiful and glorious creation. The boundless joy I feel, the pride that warms my spirit, seeing it written across your heart! Do you remember, Annona, when I summoned you into existence? I remember. How could I forget? Before flesh wrapped your bones, before your entities were placed within you, before your lungs inhaled my Spirit's breath, you were engraved on the palms of my hands.

I *knew* you.

I knew your name, I set the colours of your eyes, and I designed who you would be, sweet Annona.

With great joy and satisfaction I lifted my finger as I sculpted flesh to bone. You materialized into your physical being. But, before your ribcage closed, as an artist carves their signature into their masterpiece, so I carved my Signature across your heart. My Signature, my beloved, claiming you as Mine.

As a mother watches over her child, so I've watched over you. Born into the Ends of the Earth, you have longed for meaning and purpose, for a call on your life. For countless rotations around the sun you wondered what your Marking would be. You saw the crowd before you, their Markings becoming their identities—the very essence of who they are. They have become consumed and enslaved by the desire of purpose, they have concentrated all efforts on seeking significance. They fail to see that their heart, my Signature, satisfies all longings.

I watched you, Annona, as you tirelessly searched the Ends of the Earth for your Relics; traveling across mountains and seas in hopes of uncovering your Marking. I watched you, child, as you sat, worn and defeated, on the cusp of giving up, wondering if you had it wrong all along. I rejoiced with you, my daughter, when you uncovered your first Relic in the Land of Heat: nothing but a rock to remind you of the importance of serving the least of these. Closer than a brother, more dear than a friend—I've not left you.

When you accepted the invitation from the Painter in pursuit of your earthly Marking, all of Love Conquers All roared with celebration. That day solidified your choice: you would give your life to the releasing of Love Conquers All to the Ends of the Earth.

With the Painter's breath against your chest the word Harvester revealed, and yes, a Harvester you would be! Not only for a yield, but, my child, you would be a Harvester for Me, bringing my crowd out of suffering and into my Love.

When you set off to the Land of the Rolling Hills I heard your songs. I listened to your prayers. I saw your acts of kindness. I felt your gratitude at the creation around you. I forgave the errors you made. I knew who you needed to be with. I knew which of the crowd would support you, strengthen you, and who would help finish the work I had begun in you and bring it to fruition.

But, they came. The powers of darkness. Twisting and manipulating, they changed my truths ever so slightly so as to go undetected, but an endless chasm of suffering is what brewed beneath. Separating you from your Signature, in a culture where your identity is embedded in your capabilities, caused it to become evermore tied with what your hands, your heart, and your mind could do. The worth of my Signature never changed, but your Marking was all you saw. My Signature was hidden under false assumptions of the value you thought I had in you.

Child, could you not perceive it? My Signature is perfect *as is*. My Signature stands alone: not one letter more, not one less. *Exactly* as you are you are significant to me. I know who you are, and I know where you are going. Confidently, I have given you the Signature of royal priesthood.

Yet, the crowd and Marked are deeply confused by the purpose of a Marking: it was never about what you could do. Never about Relics or Markings, about production and value, about significance or worth.

It always, invariably, was about my Signature across your heart.

My distinction.

Whose you are, not *who* you are.

Mine.

So, when the physical world came crumbling down around you and your chest's Marking no longer aligned with what you were doing, you felt as if I had abandoned you, believing I could no longer use you.

No longer use you? Unlovable? A failure?

Oh, my child! How I longed to wrap you in my arms, to hold you until your spirit and soul came back into cadence with Me.

My child, my daughter, my friend, you are perfectly loved, unquestionably accepted, with the utmost value, worth more than any effort of sacrifice you could offer. You are unconditionally loved.

Yet, you sank into a world of darkness and mourned as if I had left you.

Here, Annona! Here! I am here!

The lies, the skewed beliefs—you sank and sank and sank. With the loss of your identity to service, my Signature became obscured. Yet, this underlying, under-the-skin, bone deep, cut-through-the-marrow truth would have set you free!

For a time, I watched you struggle. For a season, I heard your pain. The darkness cannot consume you, child, you are Mine.

As a great act of love, I will remind you of the Signature across your heart. I will remind you that you could never be forgotten. I will show you that your Marking cannot be sustained without my Signature. Child, my child! I will establish my truth. I will set you back on course.

My Annona, my beloved, from this day on, your existence will go forth from the Signature across your heart.

30

THE GERBERA DAISY

Like the sunlight breaking through the clouds after a treacherous storm, she sensed an emotion she had not experienced in many seasons: joy. It was like cold water being poured over her head, flowing down her shoulders, her legs, and to the tips of her feet. The healing waters extinguished the flames of anger that had been smouldering within her bones for much too long.

She followed the form's heart as it steadily beat, the word "Mine" stretching and collapsing with each rhythmic pump.

Expanding and collapsing—thump thump—Mine, Mine. Mine, Mine.

She felt her own heart beating inside her chest, experiencing all-consuming joy inside her heart. Joy rushed through her blood to permeate every pore, muscle, and organ, restoring life to her flesh and bones.

The Artist fixed His gaze on Annona. Annona knew He saw the truth sink into her bones, as His lips developed into a smile. This newfound grace forced the anger she had been harbouring to seep out of her pores and heal the cuts in her heart that the ache had caused. From within her flowed new blood, new life, and a new song. It was renewing her, restoring her, and healing her; a flood had been released in the wasteland.

The Artist slowly released the skin from His fingertips. The skin, like a wave spreading itself along the shore, found the opened cavity and sealed itself. The Mark, Harvester, once again clear across the Form's chest. Tenderly, He withdrew His hand and stepped back from the Form. The Form smiled at the Artist. Once more it looked at Annona, her smile as glorious as a full, golden moon on a starless night. Annona smiled at the Form as tears of healing filled her eyes. The Form looked to the sky, and suddenly evaporated into a cloud of dust, starting from the top of her head to the bottom of her soles. The dust twirled as it lifted to the heavens.

She watched the Artist as He stared into the sky, His lips smiling as if He was holding the smallest secret.

Annona's crying slowed. Swallowing, she waited for the Artist's words. The Artist looked over the Altar, His eyes searching the wooden giants that surrounded them.

"Every being was created by Me, the Sculptor, for I am the Creator, and what you saw is My Signature which I leave on my most beloved creation, the crowd. Before I ever called you into existence, I inscribed My Signature that identifies your heart as Mine. I gave, and I continue to give this Signature freely to every beating heart that enters the Ends of the Earth."

The Artist folded His hands in front of Him. Looking to the heavens He spoke, "It is through the sacrifice of My Son, the Potter, that I give this Signature. Before His sacrifice was given, there was a separation between Artist and crowd. Now, there is none. The Marking that was given during your ceremony is for those who choose to live their lives following Me on the Ends of the Earth, here and now."

The Artist paused, His gaze returning to Annona. He stepped closer to her, both His hands laid across His heart.

"Your calling, your *one and only command*, is to live your life in sound peace, knowing *you are Mine*," He drew His hand to point to her heart, "and that *I am yours.*" He clasped His hand as He beat it twice across His heart.

"This truth is cardinal to your existence, and it desires to be the unshakeable, uncrackable, unwavering foundation you set yourself on. *Everything else* is secondary to this. Your greatest triumphs, your most pure ambitions, unbeatable talents, heartbreaking failures, unspeakable disappointments, and your saddened abandonment—they hold no power over you. Most certainly, victories and failures: they do not define you. This is not how I see you, for your accomplishments carry no significance in the value you have to Me. When I look at you Annona, I see what is engraved across your heart: My unremovable Signature. For Me, it is the only Marking I see.

"If you live your life knowing your identity is forever established in Me, no matter where you are, or what you are doing, you will not fear failure or disappointing Me. You will live knowing everything, both the big and the small, the beautiful and the ugly, the tedious and the exciting—*all of it* is used for My glory, *for you are Mine.*"

Annona weighed His words, processing what He had revealed. An immediate sense of fear surged in her, "If I find my identity in You, and the Marking across my chest does not define who I am, then what am I to do with my hands, my heart, and my mind? My greatest efforts will always fall short to the Signature across my heart. What's the point in giving myself to something?"

The Artist returned His hands to His side. "Let Me ask you this. Why do you feel so much conviction to help the oppressed?"

She paused before responding, images of the children from the Land of Heat came to the forefront of her mind. "Because, I admit that my culture and lifestyle is responsible for their oppression. We have muted their voices. How can you see the brokenness and suffering and not feel compelled to give yourself to fighting it?"

"There, that's it!" He exclaimed, raising His hand to the air. "In the witnessing of the brokenness that is found in the Ends of the Earth, you feel something stirring—" His voice quieted as he motioned her to finish the sentence.

"Something stirring in my chest ... in my heart ... to do something about it. To devote myself—my time, energy, resources, care, love, and ultimately, my life—on behalf of the hungry. To satisfy the needs of the oppressed ..." Annona was quoting the Book of Suneidésis.

"... then your light will rise in the darkness and your night will become like noonday." The Artist finished the phrase, His eyebrow lifted as He smiled at Annona. "You see, you are compelled to bring light, to bring repair into the Ends of the Earth where there is brokenness."

The Artist turned, walking away from Annona. Before He stepped through the circle of scorched earth, the grass revived in front of Him, returning to its former lushness and verdant colour. Just outside the ring, a new patch of wildflowers burst from the soil, from stem to full bloom. He plucked a single flower out of the earth, holding the stem steadily between His forefinger and thumb.

The gerbera daisy was scarlet red, with a snowy white centre. He twirled the stem between His fingers. As the flower twirled, the colours blurred, making an illusion of flowing into one another. He held the flower to His nose, inhaling the scent. A slight smile developed on His lips while He lowered the flower to the centre of His chest.

"Many seasons ago My creation was perfect. My creation did not lack in anything. It did not understand the feeling of absence because it had everything it ever needed." The Artist brought the flower to His nose a second time, His eyes closed as He inhaled its perfume. "My crowd lived from their heart's Signature, their identity established in Me. They were whole." He spun the blossom between His fingers, His eyes settling on the delicacy of the flower.

"How could one think something was missing, when they possessed everything? It was through this deception, the twisting of the truth, that they stopped identifying themselves through their heart's Signature and identified themselves with something else." The Artist's mouth quivered as His voice cracked with pain. "What was once whole became broken."

He took the tip of a crimson petal, swiftly plucking it from the wooly white centre. He sighed as His eyes examined the entire flower. He presented the gerbera daisy to Annona. She took the flower into her hands, eyes fixed on the space where the single petal had been plucked. Even though the flower still possessed beauty, the void where the petal was robbed from was now the focal point of both of their attention. The Artist held the lone petal in the palm of His hand, held so that Annona could see it.

"One looks at this flower and knows it is missing its true beauty, that the potential of the flower is not what it was meant to be. One gazes at the flower and knows it could, rather, it should have greater beauty. This perception of brokenness is innate in you; My Signature over each and every heart is a Marking of perfection, the essence of a being—a soul—cries out to the Ends of the Earth to be repaired, mended, unified, reconciled, and whole." The Artist stepped closer to Annona, the petal remaining in the centre of His palm.

"I have what the Ends of the Earth is missing, and I use the crowd of the Marked to be the ambassadors of healing, mending, and fixing. I allow you to join in this work because this kind of work fills something deep within your heart."

He looked earnestly at Annona, carefully taking up the petal and placing it in her hands. The Artist nodded at the flower. Annona took the petal carefully between her fingers and tried to set the petal back into the space where it had been plucked. The petal did not attach, not even for a second. Instead, it lofted down into the grass below.

Annona gasped as she stooped down to the ground, chasing the fallen petal. She sifted through the thick blades of grass to retrieve it. The Artist met her at the ground, crouching closely beside her.

"When they thirst, and you go to collect water, come to Me, the Reservoir that quenches all thirst. When they are hungry, and you go to break bread, come to Me, the Bread that ends hunger. When they're wounded, and you go to find aid, come to Me, the Healing that soothes all who are suffering. Your dependence on Me will set your feet in your heart's Signature. Not the one across your chest, and not in what your hands, your heart, and your mind can do."

Annona found the petal among the blades of grass. She picked it out, passing it to the Artist. The Artist lifted the petal between His thumb and index finger, raising it level to her eyes.

"I am the Healer, the Mender, the Author of Restoration. When you identify that it is *Me* who is conducting the reconciling, and it is not within your own strength, we can bring about true healing—not temporary, not for a season, but eternal. My healing starts on the Ends of the Earth and sets forth into the Land of Love Conquers All."

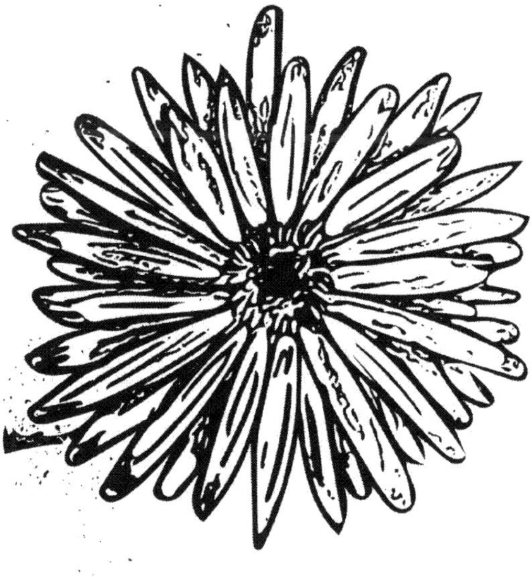

The Gerbera Daisy

The Artist extended the petal to Annona. She glanced at the Artist, then back to the petal. She took it carefully between her finger and thumb. The Artist wrapped His hand around Annona's, placing His fingers carefully over hers. Annona held the flower and the petal closely together, but, before setting them together, waited to feel pressure from

His hand. She raised her head to look at the Artist. He met her eyes with kindness, a smile formed across His face. Annona sensed the nudge of His hand. Together, they led the petal to the centre of the flower. The moment the base of the petal touched the flower's centre, the petal attached itself to the core, returning the flower to its former beauty.

Annona, guided by the Artist, carefully withdrew her hand. She beamed with joy as she spun the blossom in the same manner the Artist had done, bringing the flower to her nose as she treasured its aroma. The Artist laughed as He stood up, offering His hand, raising her to her feet.

"You ask what's the purpose in doing what your hands, your heart, and your mind give itself naturally to, when your first and foremost is to live from your heart's Signature?" The Artist dropped His eyes to the flower, "It's the opportunity to take part in the repairing and the mending of the Ends of the Earth; to bring reconciliation to the brokenness, and in doing so, bring you closer to Me. You will become dependent on me. You are to offer me your hands, your heart, and your mind in every situation you're in, to any individual who is before you, in every place that your feet stand. Giving your hands, your heart, and your mind is a response to My love. That is why you choose to give them as a selfless deed."

Annona nodded her head in agreement.

"This might scare you, Annona, because you now realize your works and efforts do not set you apart. Your greatest achievements will consistently fall short of the Signature across your heart," the Artist said, His voice so calm it soothed Annona's soul.

"Once you sincerely believe what I am saying is true, there can be no Marking that is given to you across your chest that is greater than someone else's given Marking. There is no land that will fulfill your purpose. Your purpose is found by you making a decision to give your hands, your heart, and your mind to Me in *everything* you undertake, and in *anything* that is presented before you. When you live knowing you are Mine, nothing you do will be done in vain—everything contributes to the defining of your Masterpiece. The two identities will be in constant conflict with each other, fighting for where you elect to dig your stakes, but the word that was engraved across your heart *must* win. *Every time*." He set His hand over her chest, centred to her beating heart. Annona rested her hand on top of His.

"Why did the Painter give me the Marking of Harvester?" Annona asked, her hands falling to her sides.

The Artist grinned at her. "The Painter is Me and I am Him. I gave you the Marking. You will always find it most instinctual to harvest, as this is what your hands, your heart, and your mind give itself naturally to, given the gifts and the talents We gave you. That is good. I want you to carry out projects you enjoy and that you find contentment in: extending mercy and goodness into the Ends of the Earth. But, when the season changes, or I offer something unfamiliar in your path and your heart is not in it, or your mind refuses to give, did I make a mistake in the Marking given to you, or the place in which I have set you?"

The Artist shook His head. "I don't make mistakes, Annona. Everything I do can be worked together for good whether you decide to follow the Marking across your chest or not. Ultimately, you have the choice whether you will *allow Me* to use your works, no matter what they are, for good. I can't force you to do that—I won't." The Artist paused as His jaw tightened, forcing a swallow.

"Do you remember when you shared your Relics with the Painter?"

"Of course," she replied. How could she forget the excitement of that long awaited day?

"So, you remember when the Painter told you that He must tell you something—something that might not be easy to hear?"

Annona's brow furrowed, her nose scrunched up. She recalled the moment, when the Painter explained to her that there were powers of darkness that would continue to pursue her.

The Artist laughed. "Yes, and you gave Him that exact face."

"Yes, I remember," Annona grinned sheepishly.

The Artist nodded. "Well, I too need to tell you something—something that might not be easy for you to hear."

31

RELEASING

"Annona, this might not be easy for you to hear, but listen when I say this; I want you to hear it so you can release yourself from a burden you placed upon yourself. I love the crowd more than you do, and I care for their needs more deeply than you can imagine. It's not a matter of comparison because there is none to be had. Worrying about the needs of those who are hurting is not your burden to bear, it has always been mine."

His hands rested on her shoulders. "I never inflict poverty onto them, rather suffering was released the moment that the crowd first rejected their hearts' Signature. To you I gave the privilege of coming alongside those in poverty for several seasons: to witness gratefulness and resilience. You may only choose to be with them for a limited season. However, I am with them constantly, eternally, whether the Marked choose to follow the Marking across their chest or not."

He dropped His hands from her shoulders, offering a hand for her to grasp. Annona placed her hold in His. He looked deep into her eyes, searching them. "Annona, do they pray to you or Me when they have needs? Do they urge you to give them strength, or for Me to give them strength? I would never demand of you something that is impossible for you to give. You need to trust Me with their needs and wellbeing, for I am closer to their suffering than you can understand."

Annona dropped her head, her eyes falling shamefully to the ground. He gently tilted her chin up to face Him. When her eyes met His, she saw they were glazed with tears. He took her hand back into His and exhaled out of His nose—His eyes still searching hers.

"When an opportunity is placed before you to fill a role, to accept a title, perhaps to perform in something different and unfamiliar than before—ask Me if that is something I have in store for you. Ask Me if I want you to fill that space. The yoke of the Potter is easy, and His burden is light. There will be seasons of voids. The harvest is plentiful, but the workers are few. It is not your burden to harvest tenfold, it is your burden to *stop* producing with your hands and to be still—by *starting* to pray on your knees. Ask Me to send more: urge the Painter to stir up the calling of the Marked and the Artist to swell in the divisions where the workers are not. Trust in Me."

Annona recalled the memories of her planting in the Land of Rolling Hills: the grueling work she did, the bitterness that welled in her heart when she took on the extra title.

"There would have been gaps," Annona said.

"Yes."

She shook her head quickly—He wasn't understanding what she was trying to say.

"That means that there would have been an even smaller yield, even less of the crowd receiving food."

The Artist breathed in slowly, nodding His head in agreement.

"But—aren't we to serve You? To model after the Potter? He always served!"

Crows feet appeared around His eyes as He squinted. "The Marked love to mention His servitude, but what of the times He disappeared to the mountains? The times when He would get inside a boat to escape from the crowd? The multiple years of work *before* starting His ministry?" The Artist pulled on His apron, patting some of the dried clay away. "He was all powerful: had full access to unlimited authority. He Could summon anything, and everything He needed. But, what did He model for the Marked?"

The Artist smiled before answering.

"He modeled making a choice to rest. To rely on Me and My timing. To set your identity in Me, not in your Marking, and not in what your hands, your heart, and your mind can do."

Once again, Annona's eyes dropped, but the Artist swiftly ducked His head down, locking eyes with Annona. Annona smiled, raising her head.

"I know the intentions of your heart were pure, but you trusted in your own strength to fix something you could not. When you trust in Me it means you believe I will provide the workers needed to get the task completed. And when they don't come as quickly as you hope for, you remain in the work I give to you and trust that what is needed will be provided from Me, because you believe I am good. Trusting in Me means your significance is founded in My Signature, *not* what is across your chest. The heart's Signature is what sustains the Marking. Much like the soil sustains the wooden giant's roots, the heart's Signature sustains your second Marking."

The Artist gave Annona's hands a tight squeeze, His eyes staring deeply into hers.

"Annona, *the first sustains the second.*"

Annona pulled her eyes from Him, searching the charred grass in front of her. *The first sustains the second—who I am in Him is my foundation,* she told herself. *My hands, my heart, and my mind will come next.* Annona experienced a transformation within her, a weight she had been carrying and did not know how to explain, finally lifted.

"You're getting it, Annona," the Artist said, smiling with joy. "What I can promise you is that as long as you remain faithful to the mission before you and you surrender your ambitions for Mine every day, every hour, and every moment, I will use it all for My glory. Ask the Painter to help you. That is what He does. He guides, He anoints, He helps to release.

"Annona, you merely see your Masterpiece," He continued, "but I see the grand picture. I see how everything—the unseen, unnoticed, and unappreciated—comes beautifully together. That is what I do, this is why I am an Artist." He chuckled, drawing in a deep breath and stepping towards Annona.

"There is one more act we must do: a practice I ask for you to make part of your life." The Artist stepped back, placing himself beside her. "When my Son, the Potter, came to the Ends of the Earth, He remained amongst the disciples, the ones He invited to witness and join in His journey. He would break bread with them, using the time of fellowship to speak and encourage them, and to hear their hearts' cries. One night as He was sharing with them, a mother came and poured out a treasured, expensive oil, spreading it across the Potter's feet, using her hair to wipe them." Annona knew of the story, she had read it many times in the Book of Suneidésis.

"As the perfume flowed from the jar and mixed with the dust on the floor beneath the Potter's feet, it became the perfect sacrifice—a libation poured out in honour of Him. The act was done as a sacrifice, spilled out to honour Him." The Artist slipped His hand into hers.

"Your time in the Land of Rolling Hills was an offering, a libation, for Me. Your blood, sweat, tears, frustrations, joys, victories: you did none in vain. Just as some of the oil spilled onto the dirt, and perhaps she felt it missed its destiny, I invite you to surrender even the failed deeds as a beautiful offering to Me."

Annona had not grasped how rigidly she clenched on to her work; how she had often doubted if any of it was meaningful or worthwhile. She now understood that He was urging her to surrender all the uncertainty and doubt to Him, trusting that He would use it for His glory.

At the Altar, with open hands she spoke, "Artist, let all I have touched, every word of love I have spoken, every deed I have carried in kindness, and all the places in which I have fallen short and have found myself in need of your grace..." Annona paused, releasing a breath. "Let it all be returned to You. Take it as a holy sacrifice and let none of it be wasted."

The Artist took a strong whiff with His nostrils, His face brightened, and His eyes smiled. "It is finished." He reached out His arms, opening them wide.

Annona stepped into them, His arms firmly wrapped around her. Her head rested securely on His chest.

The Artist bent His head down and whispered in her ear, "I will always come for you. I will ever be there for you. Call out to Me, and I am there: not hiding, nor absent. I'm in the midst. Nothing will restrain Me from coming to you. Let not the silence frighten you, for that is where you will find My presence."

Annona squeezed Him tighter, never wanting to let go. He saturated Annona with His grace. She acknowledged a powerful sense of repentance stirring in her heart. "Forgive me, Artist. I held on to too much; I cradled my pain, and I neglected my heart's Signature. I am so sorry," she wept, her body shaking uncontrollably in His arms.

"Annona, you've been forgiven long ago," the Artist whispered.

He continued His embrace: His hands slid through her hair and His chin rested on her head. He waited until their breathing was in sync, then gently relaxed His grip.

"You've hidden your Masterpiece in secrecy. Do not keep it in the dark any longer. Your Masterpiece will go on to develop and form: changing and creating. Set it where you can view it—out of the darkness and into the light!"

He stepped back from Annona. Annona blinked with astonishment as His hands that were empty just moments ago appeared to be holding her Masterpiece. Annona felt pure elation gazing at her image. The colours had completely transformed from when she had seen it last. The design had reached an entirely different form across the canvas.

It was messy, colourful, and beautiful.

The Artist stepped toward Annona, delicately setting the canvas in her arms. Annona took the Masterpiece, beaming at the strokes of paint, the blending of the colours, the unique definition of the piece. The Artist leaned over and kissed the centre of her forehead. "I love you," He whispered.

She looked up at Him once more, studying His face, His kindness, His love. "I love You, too."

She got lost in her Masterpiece, examining every stroke and splatter of paint. She looked up from the painting to the Artist, only to find that He was gone. What He left behind was His peace, and she was profoundly immersed in it.

Annona laughed, her arms fully extended so she could take the Masterpiece all in. She sat down in the field, breathing in the tranquility she had missed for much too long.

A few hours passed, which seemed like minutes to her, while she sang choruses of praise, recalling her anthems and battle cries. Sensing she was ready, she rose to her feet, recognizing a new strength that was restored, steadying her once tired knees. She was ambitious to establish a new day with joy.

As she was soaking in her newfound strength, she felt the warmth of the ground on the soles of her feet. Annona looked down, and to her awe, her shoes had been removed. She knew she had been standing on holy ground.

Part VI

The Heart of Flesh

"And I will give you a new heart, and a new spirit I will put within you. And I will remove the heart of stone from your flesh and give you a heart of flesh."

Ezekiel 36:26

32

RESTORATION

"Yes, can I have a medium coffee in a mug for here? Black. I'll take the roast from 'Land of Rolling Hills', thank you."

Annona softly placed her wallet on the counter, fidgeting with the zipper as the server nodded and reached below the bar, producing a ceramic mug from the collection hidden beneath the counter.

Annona turned herself slightly, leaning on the counter. She inhaled, taking in the aromas of the dark brewed coffee, the scent of the grassy teas, and the sweetness of the doughy pastries. A few hours from now, upon leaving the coffee shop, her shirt and jeans would give off the aroma of coffee—the well-trained nose knowing where she had been.

Annona made this coffee shop, The Bower, her second home, frequenting in-between shifts at the Garden and on days when she wasn't required at work. She made it her mission to come every opportunity she had, knowing that within a brief time, The Bower wouldn't be accessible to her anymore.

A few moments passed as the server returned to Annona with the coffee. "Here you are. Sugar and cream are on the counter by the window, as I'm sure you know," the server said smiling as she carefully passed her the mug, the steam swirling like a ribbon, drifting lazily.

Annona wrapped her fingers around the sturdy handle. The coffee rippled within the mug. Golden crema splashed against the borders of the ceramic walls. She scanned the area behind her for a chair, hoping to find her favourite table available. It was a small table with two seats aligned against the window, allowing her both the view of the outdoors and of the patrons within the coffee shop. In her bag she brought her notepad, her Book of Suneidésis, and her small radio. The coffee shop was tranquil today. Only a few of Guardian's Ridge's artists and writers were scattered amongst the tables, leaving a respectful cushion of territory among the creators. Annona found her table open, grateful for the view and for the privacy.

She set the coffee down, the ceramic clinking against the wooden table. She pulled off her satchel, placing it in the chair across from her.

Coffee at The Bower.

Sliding out her books and notepad, she reviewed the work she wanted to accomplish today. Annona had three more weeks before she would return to the Land of Rolling Hills, report to the same fields, even rent on the same street she had before.

Several rotations around the sun had passed since her encounter with the Artist at the Altar. The encounter with the Artist at the Altar had provoked Annona's Before and After: Before, she had hopelessly performed in a mistaken identity—she was never created to find her purpose in it. But, after Altar, she lived—truly lived—in the freedom and grace of her authentic identity—His Marking across her heart. She lived freely, knowing that she was His. Everything else was secondary to this.

It was at the Altar that she had sacrificed her identity as "Harvester," giving it back to the One who gave her the skills and passions for harvesting in the first place, and in return she received a life established in the freedom of her new identity.

Following the encounter at the Altar, there had been a release in her emotions. She cried more, sang more, danced more, and offered herself more grace for her mistakes. She felt she was figuring herself out for the first time, which was surprising, as she thought she already knew everything about herself.

Only a few moon cycles ago, Akim had sought Annona after returning to speak at the Gallery in Guardian's Ridge. Annona was thrilled and terrified at the same time. Annona believed that Akim wouldn't want her back, as things had ended less than ideally. But, Akim, true to his character, only received her with grace and understanding. He was elated to learn that Annona had experienced an encounter with the Artist, in which He revealed her heart's identity, in comparison to her Marking. Akim then explained to Annona that on the very day that she had unearthed the weed that had ravaged the harvest, he himself had attempted to reveal the same truth to her. If only she had known to listen! Annona knew that the posture of her hands and heart would not have received his explanation at that time. The darkness had led her to the light; and it was through brokenness that she had came into a posture ready to heal.

Without hesitation, Akim invited Annona to return to the Land of Rolling Hills. As soon as the invitation to return to the fields had left Akim's lips, Annona's mind was flooded with thousands of emotions and ideas reminiscent of the old Annona who had left for the Land of Rolling Hills many seasons ago—and they all desired a stake in her heart. Dismayed by the influx of the memories, she paused, knowing that she could not give Akim an immediate answer. At that time, Annona had completely surrendered the idea of returning to the Land of Rolling Hills. With the guiding help of the Painter, she had allowed the Artist to be the King of her heart—not her dreams, not her calling. Akim told her to take all the time she needed, leaving the invitation open for when she received her answer from the Artist.

Annona brought the dark liquid to her lips, and as it rippled against the rim of the mug she blew the steam away. She took a small sip, burning the tip of her tongue. Carefully, slowly, she placed the mug beside her notebook as she glanced at the crowd dispersed around the coffee shop. She smiled as a few made eye contact with her; some were strangers, others, frequenters like herself. When she looked to the far corner of the room, her heart dropped. Her heart saw first what her eyes perceived second. She felt her stomach turn upside down and a cold whisper rushed down her spine.

It was Jore.

His eyes latched on her, the edge of his mouth slowly raised. He bit his lip, his eyes dropped to his coffee as he protectively wrapped his fingers around the mug. He dipped his head, sighed, and put on his backpack, tucking in his chair and grabbing his drink as he walked toward Annona.

Annona shifted in her chair, unaware of the uncensored expression on her face. Her mouth dangled open like a saucer, and her eyes stung, brimmed with tears.

She forced a swallow, her hands wrapping around her mug. The heat of the coffee too hot for her grip, but nevertheless she kept it there. The sting of the heat stole her attention from the sting that was throbbing in her heart.

"Can I sit here?" he asked, his voice raspier, deeper, than she had remembered from the fields.

"Of course," Annona said, her hand needing to release the heat. She twirled the mug with her fingertip as Jore lifted Annona's satchel out of the chair, lightly leaning it against the wall underneath the table. He offered a tight smile as he shimmied off his backpack, ever cautious not to spill his drink. He set his mug directly in front of Annona's coffee, placed his backpack on the floor, and lowered himself smoothly into the chair.

She had thought of calling him hundreds, maybe even thousands of times in the past several rotations around the sun, especially when she accepted Akim's offer. But, every time she went to pick up the phone, she would lose her courage. He had taken off without informing her, without saying goodbye, so why would he want to hear from her now?

Annona raised her eyes to his. He was already staring at her, his gaze searching her eyes as if for a clue as to what was racing through her mind. He chewed the inside of his lip, a tear streaking down his cheek. Abruptly, he used the back of his hand to wipe it away. She could sense the tension: the energy of anxiousness and anticipation, like watching the tails of fireworks launched into the night sky, not knowing when they will explode.

"In my mind, I've known what I needed to express to you, to clarify—even justify—my decisions, but in this moment, seeing you ... I've got nothing—" His voice broke. He tried starting again, but stopped as he couldn't speak without choking on his words. He shook his head, dropping his eyes as tears broke away: tiny droplets chased after the first, absorbing it, flowing even faster down his cheek.

Annona felt it, everything he was feeling, in her. The time lost, the suffering endured, the questions unanswered, the unrelenting shame: she had felt it too.

She reached across the table, taking his hand in hers as a tear slipped past her cheek. Her own sudden reaction of grace surprised her. In her mind, she had imagined yelling at him, demanding for him to understand the pain he had put her through. Instead, she was moved by grace, the effects of the Painter had overtaken her.

Jore focused on her hand over his, his thumb pressing on her limp fingers. "I was young, inexperienced, and proud. I was jealous of titles, Elders, and recognition. When Mirmah came, I was already in too deep. The feelings of jealously and dissension were already in my heart—it was Mirmah's listening ear that misled me," he said.

Annona nodded, recalling the time she had looked into the fields and the shock when she saw no one was there.

"But even so, Annona, it's not an excuse. No one forced me to leave. No one was taking advantage of me. I led myself to that position and I knew what I was doing."

Jore raised his stare to meet hers, his eyes glazed with tears, lips pressed tightly. She studied him, honestly, deeply, looking past the stubble on his cheeks and his crescent moon eyes.

He was Jore: her first friend in the Land of Rolling Hills, her mentor in the fields, and her companion when life was difficult. She sensed the walls around her heart crack, faintly, giving way for emotion to seep in.

"After I left, I returned to my village. It was bad, Annona. I thought I had lost everything. I was so ashamed, so consumed in my guilt ... I was rudderless." He slowly drew his hands from Annona's, taking his mug back into his grip as he took a draw of its warm liquid. He looked out the window, watching the crowd lazily cross the street.

"The Shepherd at the Gallery intervened. He allowed me a few moon cycles to wallow in my self pity, although I'm sure he was secretly hoping I'd snap out of the shallowness by myself. But, when I proceeded to drown into the third moon cycle, he put a stop to it. He mentored me, guided me, helped me to own my mistakes, and reminded me of all that the Artist has done for me. It's been hard, but I'm learning my part, seeing the importance of giving my hands, my heart, and my mind to everything I do."

"Yes, living from your heart's Signature," Annona added.

Jore's eyes widened, then quickly tightening, he asked, "Wait, did the Shepherd talk to you, too?"

Annona breathed deeply, inhaling the Painter, exhaling the Sculptor and the Potter, before responding. "I learned it from the Artist. We had an encounter several seasons back when things were difficult for me."

Jore looked surprised, then his face transitioned into shame as he fidgeted with his mug, quickly withdrawing his hands and rubbing them against his legs.

"Did I do that to you?" Jore asked, hardly above a whisper. "Did I make things difficult for you?"

"No, I did it to myself, when I identified the essence of who I was in my Marking, and not in the Artist," Annona said. It was difficult to own her contribution in the breakdown of her dreams, but wrapping her identity in her Marking was on her—Jore had nothing to do with that.

Jore nodded his head slowly, pensively, before returning his eyes to hers.

"I am sorry, Annona. For not seeking you for help, for not saying goodbye, for damaging the harvest."

Annona gave a slight smile, "Jore, the harvest carries on, with or without us. It's not our harvest, it's the Artist's. I am grateful for the time we had together, and the friendships we made ... that we were part of something much greater than ourselves." As the words left Annona's mouth, she knew they were true.

"I didn't tell you about Mirmah, or about my resentment toward the Elders, because I was afraid if I did, I would provoke you to become resentful too," Jore said. "I hope you understand; I thought I was looking out for you. I'm sorry for any part I had in you leaving the harvest."

Annona remained silent for a moment before slowly nodding her head, biting the inside of her lower lip.

"What's done is done, Jore. I hope you don't carry the burden of how you left. I've forgiven you—and you know the Artist has forgiven you. And, through this whole process, I've learned to forgive myself."

Annona took her coffee, sipping on the liquid. The server came over, pouring refills into both of their mugs. Thanking her, Jore continued to look out the window. He began flicking the rim of his drink. The sound of his nail hitting the rim of his cup mimicked a timer in sync to Annona's escalating pulse. She felt the urge to ask the question lodged in her soul. It was the question she had been wanting to ask him for many rotations around the sun, one that she had avoided, fearing his response. She'd lost count of the times she hung the receiver before ever having the courage to dial his number. But, now, with him sitting there in front of her, it was time.

"Jore?"

"Yes?"

"I have to ask you something."

"Okay."

"Was my error with the Roshgephen weed the root of your bitterness? Because I've thought about it, and I can't recall anything 'off' before that event."

Jore stopped flicking his mug: the absence of the sound foreshadowing his answer. Now Annona's ears rang to the rhythmic beat of her heart. His eyes snapped to the drink in his hands. He pursed his lips, and, after a beat, lifted his eyes to her. A pause. Neither one of them moved.

"Honestly, Annona ... yes. Up to that point, I had fostered some negative thoughts in my head, but I hadn't acted on them. I hadn't even spoken them aloud. The Roshgephen weed was what triggered my anger. I spoke with Mirmah a few weeks after it had happened, and shortly after that, I started to seek out other disgruntled workers."

Annona chewed on the inside of her lip, unable to look him in the eyes. Her fear was coming true: she had played a part in Jore's demise.

"Annona, the weed was a mistake, an accident. I know you didn't do it on purpose. It isn't an excuse for my behaviour. I see that now through the guidance of the Shepherd. At that time, I thought all of it was justified: my anger, my resentment towards the Elders, and the frustrations with my Marking. My bitterness was because of my own selfish ways. I wanted to hold someone else accountable, and I refused to look at myself as being in the wrong."

Annona nodded her head slowly, wrapping her hands around the mug as she took in Jore's explanation.

"For what it's worth, I am sorry," Annona said.

Jores eyes crinkled, unable to meet hers. He shifted in his seat, leaning his crossed arms on the table. Raising his vision to hers, he gave a half smile.

"Thank you, Annona."

The smile slowly grew, and as the smile radiated from his face, she was reminded of the times she would spot Jore's white smile amongst the golden harvest.

Annona gave a small grin, thankful she was finally able to release the weight that she had been carrying within her since her time in Desert's Stone. She was thankful to have her friend back.

"Wow, the Artist sure has worked on us, eh?"

"He sure has," Annona replied.

"Would've been nice to have known all this stuff before, you know, before the meltdowns and all," Jore said, a look of mischievousness forming on his face.

Annona burst with laughter. She took her mug, cautiously taking a sip. The temperature had dropped to the heat she could enjoy without burning her tongue.

Jore stayed for a few hours longer, catching up with Annona. Trudging through the heavy, they reached the lighthearted: the joy that is exclusively experienced by those who have been beaten and struck down, but not destroyed. The elation that is experienced by the Marked, who, without doubt, are certainly convinced that they are loved, accepted, accounted for, and safely held in the hands of the Artist—His Signature etched across their hearts.

Jore promised to remain in touch, even inviting her to the Land of Heat to visit the fields in which he was planting. Annona took his contact information, excited at the prospect of traveling back to the land where she had first found her Relic, the rock, that had first sparked her interest in living abroad. Jore also promised to visit the Land of Rolling Hills soon, as Akim had invited him to orientate some of the new Planters who were beginning on the fields.

When the time came for them to part, they approached the departure not as a goodbye, but rather *I'll be seeing you soon*. They both left confident knowing their paths would surely cross again.

33

FROM HIS SIGNATURE

Annona had a hard time wrapping her mind around the revelation that all the Artist ever had wanted from her was to live in her heart's identity. She understood that in any area He placed before her, the Artist would use it for His glory. No longer claiming her abilities and passions as her own identity, she determined instead to do her best to always give her deeds and work back to the Artist.

Her life had changed from the inside out, as it would when one discovers the freeing truth that one can approach Him in confidence—not because of anything one's done, but because of what He has freely given.

It took discipline to constantly surrender her desires, gifts, talents, and needs to Him. For the crowd, it is natural to want to control their lives, to desire order, and to receive what is expected. The crowd tightens their grip like vices over titles, achievements, or possessions they are given. A false sense of security takes hold, justifying their efforts with religious words like "helping," "calling," or "serving." Annona even knew many of the Marked who only knew themselves as their Marking, who failed to use the Painter to reveal the Artist's Signature. Stuck in an endless cycle of serving, they did not realize they were missing what set them apart from the crowd: the unlimited access to His Presence. They had determined the source of joy they experienced was from the fruit of their service, not from the Presence of the Artist Himself. What would happen when their serving efforts would fail to reap a harvest? Or their efforts were deemed useless? Because, inevitably, all accomplishments and materials in the Ends of the Earth will turn to dust.

Annona could now perceive the chase for significance rampant among the Marked. The core longings of belonging and purpose exploited by the deceits of the powers of darkness. Even though the Marked bear His Signature, they believe the common lie that it is not enough: a title or accomplishments will fill the void, will ensure their significance. But, even with this new title in the palm of their hand, they cannot help their wandering eyes from wanting whatever else is around them. Releasing what they've finally fought for, they try to grasp more, and the pursuit they were struggling to control now governs over them. Titles, identities, items, and possessions. The Ends of the Earth is constantly demanding a stake in their heart. But, there is a question they must ask themselves: do they truly have control? Or, is everything that has been bestowed upon them a gift to be eventually returned to the same hands that provided it? The Marked must ask themselves: can the task before me fail, and I still know that I am securely loved, significant, and chosen by the Artist?

The Painter offers so much more: a steadfast love, peace, grace, truth, joy, significance—all within their grasp, regardless of whether achievements come to fruition or not. And it is not just a superficial version of it, it is *true* grace, *true* joy, *true* peace. It requires an act of surrender, and the Painter will do the rest.

Annona was open to being stretched by the Artist: to try projects that her hands might not give themselves naturally to, to trust that in the areas where she would lack He would be evident all the more. And He was. He always showed up, filling Himself into the places where she could not. She looked to Him in giving her guidance on what to engage in next—on which role He might want her to fulfil—remembering to ask for direction instead of assuming it was all up to her to find a solution. She learned to be still and wait for His gentle touch.

Even after the defining moment with the Artist at the Altar, in the next several seasons she would spend in Guardian's Ridge, her heart would swell with sadness with the thought of the Land of Rolling Hills and the good work she was part of during that time. When she had not yet received the invitation from Akim, she continued working at the community gardens, overseeing the production and layout of the plants and vegetation. Sometimes she would listen to the Elder Harvesters and Planters at the Gallery, ones who had spent the majority of their lives in places all over the Ends of the Earth. As they would speak of the work they were accomplishing, Annona's heart would swell with longing and grief. She wondered if the Artist would give her the opportunity to go back, or if the Land of Rolling Hills would be something forever in her past. At times, she felt as if she were going backwards in her grief, like her life would never be fully normal again.

But, it wasn't true. With the passing of each day, even if the progress was small, the hurt stung a little less as the healing waters reached the areas of her soul that were wounded. The grief did not consume her. The anger would come and disappear, and the ache was losing its intensity. She granted her heart to grieve, but all the while she praised the Artist for the wonderful work He was doing through her. She was determined to celebrate the little victories, slowing her pace, grateful for the harvest she was reaping in Guardian's Ridge.

She continued to ask Him to be the King of her heart: to only allow Him on the throne, not her calling nor her dreams. It had to be Him, because everything else would fail. Everything else would eventually hurt. *Only He* could provide the security that was needed in each moment.

When she was set to return to the Land of Rolling Hills the next day, she was different. Gone was the old Annona, who was wrapped in an identity she could never achieve. The way she spoke to the crowd, her expectations of herself, the joy that was bursting from her bones, this became her new norm. The Artist had taken her to the next level in life, allowing her to live from her true identity: His.

The greatest meaning of all was the revealing of His Signature across her heart—this first and foremost, she was His. Nothing that anyone could do, not her lack of motivation, or tasks attempted or failed could ever remove the Signature from her heart. As difficult as it all had been—the anger and the ache, the burn out, the misery—she'd repeat it all ten-thousands time over just to discover who she was in Him. When she lived from this truth, Angō was easily defeated; The Brothers were not a reason to be fearful, but to be brave in what the Artist would reveal; Yirah retreated; Kahcash possessed no true power; and Perispaó was nowhere to be found.

During her time in the community gardens, and around Guardian's Ridge, Annona no longer wore shirts that covered her Marking, but showed "Harvester" proudly. Each day she was determined to harvest whatever good that was placed in front of her and to give it back to the Artist as a sacrifice. She desired to encourage others, just as she had been encouraged, to know their identity was not grounded in their Marking, rather, what was etched across their hearts.

It was through the darkness, through the blackest nights, the pains unimaginable, and the loneliness unfathomable that Annona—through the Artist—unearthed the treasures of darkness, the greatest of riches stored in secret places.

Annona sat within the faded ring of charred grass. Her hands were ready to return to the fields, her heart confident in His Signature, her mind full of anticipation of what the next chapter of her life would bring. The next morning she would leave for Desert's Stone in the Land of Rolling Hills: her life packed in bags, her soul ready to go. She needed to set her feet back to the Altar one last time to remind her hands, her heart, and her mind what all of this was for.

The wind flowed through her hair as it stirred the wooden giants to sway and bow in the winds. The sun gently kissed her face. Her toes sunk into the deep grass.

"Artist," Annona said, wiping her hair away from her face, "for the past several seasons, I have abided in what You've placed before me, giving all I am as a response to your love. Tomorrow, I will return to the Land of Rolling Hills, because You have asked me to go." Annona paused, lifting herself to her feet.

"The truth is, I am scared that I will forget. I am scared I will place my identity back into what is across my chest." Annona felt a pang in her heart. She sighed, tucking her hands into her pockets. She strode a few steps forward, towards a patch of wild flowers. A white and red flower, one identical to the flower the Artist had used to explain her desires to repair the world, stood before her, bending with the grass as the winds rushed through like waves. She bent down, plucking the flower from the grass bed.

She brought it to her nose, the smell reminding her of the moment with the Artist: Him urging her to ask of Him first.

My Signature comes first, Annona. The first sustains the second.

A single tear streaked past her cheek. Her fears had no authority. Flesh for flesh, pound for pound, ounce for ounce, *her heart was His.*

"You will be with me. Help me, each and every day, to set my feet on my heart's Signature," Annona whispered, the posture of her soul on its knees. "Artist, I am where you have sent me. I am loving who You have put in front of me. I am giving to them what You are asking of me, Your servant is willing. Here I am, use my hands, my heart, and my mind; I am all Yours."

And so it would be.

The End,
Her new beginning.

Acknowledgements

It takes a village.

The angry notes scribbled in haste when I first returned from Honduras became the origin of this book. Like oxygen needed to sustain a flame, so were the laments of my undoing, feeding the belly of the fires of anger and ache. Even as I began to type these words on my keyboard, I did not possess the answers to my incessant confusion nor did I bear within me the healing waters needed to diminish the fires of my anger and ache. But, I trusted that the Holy Spirit would whisper them to me—trusting that He would pour them out. And so He did.

Ever prominent, as I worked through the conversations between the Artist and Annona, the Holy Spirit gave me the answers to her—my—questions, pain, and hurt. Although I was the instrument, I accept no possession of the words written; I give it back to Him, to God, who simply used me as the object with which He composed the words, truths, and healing. Just as an artist uses his paintbrush to lay the colour, so did He use me to release what only He could say—what only He could do. But, as the story developed to the final draft, there were many individuals along the journey that contributed, revised, modified, and offered valuable feedback, allowing the novel to grow into something greater than I ever could have accomplished on my own.

Jairo, my husband, who has been ever faithful, loving, and full of grace. When I mentioned to you I would write a novel about identity, you treated me as a seasoned novelist. Not once did you doubt my abilities. You reassured me, proposed questions along the way, and urged that I press deeper. For this, and for your agape love, I thank you. Throughout our journey of marriage, you have been so good to me. Together we are in pursuit of His Presence, and I couldn't be more grateful to have you leading us, our home, in this. To Abigail, my daughter who has brought so much joy, who has guided me into motherhood. I understand love so much more deeply because of you, I love you. To my brother Josiah, who listened to my initial ideas while sitting outside a crowded coffee shop; you encouraged me to write and offered wisdom beyond your years when you read the book from cover to cover. To Rebecca, you have been kind to me, empathetic, and consistent; thank you for always supporting my dreams. To my brother Jacob, who was part of my journey when we lived abroad. I don't think you will fully know how much it meant to me seeing you—my family—each day. To my wonderful married-in siblings: David, Selam, and Kara-Lee. Thank you for making my family more full, seasoned, and well-rounded. My mom, you spent hours editing, provided useful feedback and ample praise. My dad, I can consistently count on you to be in my corner. You both encouraged and supported me so deeply in this project. To my first readers: Kimberly, Sidney, and Christina. Thank you for taking the time to read my draft. Thank you for your gentle feedback—for pouring over the skeletons before the flesh.

To Gabby Duba, when you sent me those first few pages of edits, all I saw was red. Had it been an essay returned from a professor, I would have lost my courage to proceed. However, on this occasion the red symbolized progress, maturity, and hope. Progress, because my book was beginning to feel stagnate; I had taken it as far as I was capable, and your markings meant change. Maturity, because I knew after your edits the book would develop a greater sense of meaning and depth. And hope, because I had been praying for seasons to know what to do next with the draft, and God granted you the grace to edit it, and to edit it well. Thank you for giving hundreds of hours to scrutinize the perfect execution of the words, for the thoughtful comments, and for the imperative edits. I am so grateful. I don't know how I could ever repay you, but perhaps if we ever were to return to the Land of Rolling Hills, I'd take you out for unlimited coffees & desserts.

To our friends who came alongside me and my husband during our hardships, Cathy Gates and Brian Cook. You met with us when we were so shattered, unable to see up from down. My brokenness didn't scare you. My sins didn't repel you. Your tender guiding through the Holy Spirit began me on a journey of healing. Thank you for being there for the both of us, for listening to us, for guiding us. I am truly, eternally grateful. This leads me to Carsten and Linda Pellman. I don't know what would have happened to us if we had not met you. You helped us to re-establish our feet on the solid foundation of Christ. You guided us without judgment; you gave us tools to dig deeper into our marriage, and to discover God in new ways. Truly, thank you for helping me to realize my staggering confusion in my identity—for revealing the Artist's Marking across my heart. I pray and trust God will bless you tenfold.

And finally, to my friends and family in Honduras, my Land of Rolling Hills. This book couldn't have been written without my time there and the experiences I had. Thank you to all who came along in my journey.

It takes a village to raise a child. The many careful hands of guiding and teaching swoop in to gracefully mould and shape the character. So it was with this book. You will find in the pages of this book the fingerprints of those many hands of the people, my tribe, who continue to love fiercely and persistently, who remained among me when I was surrounded by darkness, who refused to let me sink into the black. You pushed me into the light, His glorious light, and for this I am ever grateful.

It took a village.

A portion of the money from each book sold will go to grass-root, Honduran run organizations and to Honduran families affected by the collateral damages of COVID-19.

Your Identity in Christ

Text has been altered from "you" and "we" to "I" and "me".

Made for Purpose

"Before I formed you in the womb I knew you, and before you were born I consecrated you; I appointed you a prophet to the nations." *Jeremiah 1:5*

"For I know the plans I have for you, declares the Lord, plans for welfare and not for evil, to give you a future and a hope." *Jeremiah 29:11*

"He chose me in Him before the foundations of the world." *Ephesians 1:4*

"But I received mercy for this reason, that in me, as the foremost, Jesus Christ might display his perfect patience as an example to those who were to believe in him for eternal life." *1 Timothy 1:12*

"So is my word that goes out from my mouth: It will not return to me empty, but will accomplish what I desire and achieve the purpose for which I sent it. You will go out in joy and be led forth in peace; the mountains and hills will burst into song before you, and all the trees of the field will clap their hands." *Isaiah 55:11-12*

Confidence in Him

"We have boldness and access with confidence through our faith in Him." *Ephesians 3:12*

"We are brought near to Him." *Ephesians 2:13*

"For by grace I have been saved through faith." *Ephesians 2:8*

"Whatever I do, work heartily, as for the Lord and not for men, knowing that from the Lord I will receive the inheritance as my reward. I am serving the Lord Christ." *Colossians 3:24*

"I will then with confidence draw near to the throne of grace, that I may receive mercy and find grace to help in times of need." *Hebrews 4:16*

"Be at rest once more, O my soul, for the LORD has been good to me. For you, O LORD, have delivered my soul from death, my eyes from tears, my feet from stumbling, that I may walk before the LORD in the land of the living... you have freed me from my chains." *Psalm 116:7-9, 16*

"He does not call me His servant, but He calls me His friend." *John 15:15*

"Even in darkness light dawns for the upright, for the gracious and compassionate and righteous person. Good will come to them who are generous and lends freely, who conducts their affairs with justice. Surely I will never be shaken; a righteous person will be remembered forever. I will have no fear of bad news; my heart is steadfast, trusting in the LORD. My heart is secure, I will have no fear; in the end I will look in triumph on my foes." *Psalm 112:4-8*

New Creation

"I am renewed in the Spirit of my mind, and I put on the new self, created after the likeness of God in true righteousness and holiness." *Ephesians 4:23-24*

"I am a chosen race, a royal priesthood, a holy nation, a people for his own possession, that I may proclaim the excellencies of him who called me out of darkness into his marvellous light. Once I was not a people, but now I am God's people; once I had not received mercy, now I have received mercy." *1 Peter 2:9*

"For from His fullness I have received, grace upon grace." *John 1:16*

"Now the LORD is the Spirit, and where the Spirit of the LORD is, there is freedom. And we, who with unveiled faces all reflect the LORD's glory, are being transformed into his likeness with ever-increasing glory, which comes from the LORD, who is the Spirit." *2 Corinthians 3:17*

"Therefore if I am in Christ, I am a new creation; the old has gone, the new has come!" *2 Corinthians 5:17*

I am not Afraid

"Fear not, for you are with me; be not dismayed, for He is my God. He will strengthen me, He will help me, He will uphold me with His righteous right hand." *Isaiah 41:10*

"For it is by grace that I have been saved, through faith — and this not from me, it is the gift of God — not by works, so that no one can boast." *Ephesians 2:8*

"For God gave me a spirit not of fear but of power and love and self-control." *2 Timothy 1:7*

"I cast all my anxieties on Him, because He cares for me." *1 Peter 5:7*

"I will not fear, because there is not fear in love, but perfect love casts out fear." *1 John 4:18*

"I will never perish...and no one will snatch me from out of His [Jesus'] hand." *John 10:28*

I have Hope

"I have this as a sure and steadfast anchor of the soul, a hope that enters into the inner place behind the curtain, where Jesus has gone as a forerunner on my behalf." *Hebrews 6:19*

"I will hold fast the confession of my hope without wavering, for He who promised is faithful." *Hebrews 10:23*

"See what kind of love the Father has given to us, that we should be called children of God; and so I am." *1 John 3:1*

"'Truly, truly,' He says to me, 'I will weep and lament, but the world will rejoice. I will be sorrowful, but my sorrow will turn into joy.'" *John 16:20*

"I wait for the LORD, my soul waits, and in His word I put my hope.

My soul waits for the LORD more than watchmen wait for the morning, more than watchmen wait for the morning. O my beloved, put your hope in the LORD, for with the LORD is unfailing love and with Him is full redemption. He himself will redeem me from all my sins." *Psalm 130:5-8*

"Let me not become weary of doing good, for at the proper time I will reap a harvest if I do not give up!" *Galatians 6:9*

Made in the USA
Columbia, SC
31 August 2020

17206163R00174